Public Stoning

PUBLIC STONING

God's Design for a Nation without Prisons

ADAM TERRELL

VOLUNTARY THEOCRACY
MOSCOW, IDAHO

Published by Voluntary Theocracy
Moscow, Idaho | voluntarytheocracy.org

Adam Terrell, *Public Stoning: God's Design for a Nation without Prisons.*

Cover design and interior graphics by Joey Nance.
Interior layout by Valerie Anne Bost.

Version: 20230704

This work is dedicated to everyone behind bars.
You have been mistreated,
and I think of myself as chained with you.
(Hebrews 13:3)

Acknowledgments

Special thanks to Dennis Bratcher
and the others who prefer to remain unnamed.
Your insights have greatly helped hone this book.

Contents

Preface

THIS BOOK IS WRITTEN AS AN EXHOR-
tation by a believer in the Lord Jesus Christ to other believers. Prison reform or abolition are not new goals, but
a complete alternative must be offered to achieve (and
radically exceed) the function prisons currently fill. It is
not enough to say what Scripture is against. With this
book I hope to offer what Scripture favors in absolute
ideals in regard to Scripture's laws for capital offenses.

By and large, God's people have rejected His law in
word and especially in deed. Most Christians in my experience would rather err on the side of not taking the
law seriously enough rather than taking it too seriously.
If anything, I want this book to err on the side of taking
God's law too seriously. Isn't that better than erring on

the side of sin? What would that look like fleshed out? If we can't answer the difficult foundational questions first, why even start to tackle the easy ones on flawed assumptions? We shouldn't start what we wouldn't want to finish when we get there.

This book is one of many needed to facilitate discussion on a complete overhaul of all of the nations' justice systems, starting with God's people having a desire to govern themselves by His law of liberty first. For while we are dead to the law's condemnation (Galatians 2:19), by our faith we establish the law (Romans 3:31). I hope to encourage deeper search into God's law. One day, even the poorest child on earth will have a deeper understanding of these matters than the most academic members of God's people today, because that child will see them practiced. We cannot expect unbelievers to move the world in this direction, so we as Christ's body must seek to govern ourselves and willing sojourners in all areas of law, ultimately culminating in this one—matters of life and death. This must begin by seeking to regain the responsibility to punish repentant believers, even those guilty of capital offenses as the Jews did in Babylonia (Ezra 7:11-27). Why has God seen fit to subject us to ungodly rulers? Is it not for our disobedience? If we turn to Him quickly, will He not restore our freedom and guard us?

Scripture provides a complete system for what we would call criminal justice. It does not stop there but goes on to detail matters of business, relationships, every kind of act, sinful and righteous, wise and foolish. Within the scope of these laws, I hope to focus exclusively on what capital offenses are in God's eyes as well as what should be done about those who do them. In regard to replacing prison with a Biblical system, the death penalty is far from all that is needed; it is simply the most foundational aspect. To completely replace prisons and their intended function of protecting and restoring cities, a system of law is required. This involves courts, judges, and officials with a functional knowledge of the law to enforce restitution (money, property, medical care), lawful slavery (as opposed to what many call "slavery" which Scripture says is the capital offense of man-stealing), marriage restrictions and mandates, bodily injury repayment, whipping, monetary fines, and the death penalty. In this book I will focus only on what I would call the most basic commandments and punishments: death penalties. And though it is true that carrying out the death penalty requires the most advanced understanding of law and a high level of responsibility, not murdering someone is one of the most basic rules of life, along with all other laws where death is the consequence for disobeying. With this thought in mind, this topic might be the most needful for adults newly entering the faith.

Relatively few people will listen to this while I'm alive. This kind of thinking needs to last and continue to grow far beyond my lifetime, and I want to give it its best chance at spreading long-term. This is not a fun subject; it is a life-giving subject.

When there's a big hole in someone's thinking, it takes a lot of mortar to fix it. This book is intended to be a complete and practical fix on the issue of execution. A single conversation or a web article would just put a quick handful of mortar in your brain (which may even get worn away again). I prefer to completely fill in the hole for you with this book to then allow your thinking on this topic to flourish. Bad ideas creep in at your weak points; they don't hit you where you're paying attention, at least not effectively. Then you can go and act on complete information immediately instead of being frozen with more questions and doubt.

If you agree with me that murder going unpunished will result in more human death and suffering, and that this is because God's word is true, then I have confidence that I can help to bring you to the same conclusion about any capital offense in God's law. And if I can get you there, I have confidence I can get you to agree that public stoning is one of only four acceptable means of execution today, the others being by burning, by the sword in war, or by excommunication. The avenger of blood in Numbers 35, Deuteronomy 19:1-13, and Joshua 20 will also be addressed.

The only way forward is through repentance. The alternative is continued bondage leading to death.

Christ's body must govern itself under its head. We must acknowledge that this includes the death penalty. We must not be content to rely on unbelievers for this task. Otherwise, we will wait for justice to be exacted on us by those who don't know God or His commandments. We must follow Zacchaeus's example of repentance. I'll explain what I mean by this further in.

If I am handling the Scriptures faithfully and skillfully like a sword, it'll cut everything it's meant to cut away and leave everything it's meant to leave. If I'm handling it improperly, assuming you are well-trained in handling God's word, it will miss you without a scratch. A well-placed strike with Scripture will sharpen my sword or cut away things from my thinking. Either way, God will be shown true and every man a liar. The final possibility is that I'm wrong, which I probably am in some part, and someone inept at handling Scripture will foolishly apply my error. In this case, let the error be known far and wide so that others will not repeat it (just like stoning is meant to spread word of deadly sin), and shame on me for teaching falsehood as truth. I bear double responsibility as a teacher.

Inspiration

I was raised in a Christian home where my father faithfully taught me the Bible for 1-2 hours daily, plus church on Sunday, plus Wednesday night Bible studies. I thought this was normal. In the course of reading the Bible, we read through all sorts of laws, some that made perfect sense and are widely practiced today. But there would always be ones that didn't make sense, sounded foreign, no one practiced, and we didn't discuss them as much. As children so often do, I learned by example. Since there was no one to model many of these laws for me, I just assumed that there was some reason that no one obeyed these laws anymore. I assumed there was some detail that I just didn't yet understand that would eventually explain it.

Early in my teens, I remember being struck by R.C. Sproul's series "The Holiness of God" and how violent God could be, which seemed at first to be overreaction on His part. But through the course of the series, they made much more sense in light of His perfection, mercy, and yet consistent hatred of evil. R.C. Sproul even went as far as pointing to the seriousness of blasphemy. He condemned it as something worthy of much more than a mere legal fine. I tucked that thought in my back pocket.

Being a homeschooling family, we had an understandable focus on American politics. I got a steady stream of political discussion growing up, and we listened to talk radio as a family (though my mom didn't like the usually confrontational aspect of it). We often discussed it in light of Scripture during car trips. We got several of our ideals from Dennis Prager, Michael Medved, and others on AM 660 KSKY. They touched (and still touch) on many moral subjects not addressed at any local body that I've ever been part of. We obviously had our agreements and disagreements with their views.

One of the downsides of listening to conservative talk radio is that, in order to be relevant to a large enough audience, it must focus on national political discussions almost completely, and very rarely state issues. It never brought county and city politics to discussion unless it tied closely into a national issue, and even then only in passing as a launchpad for wider discussion. While I agree that it's important to recognize national symptoms, focusing only on the symptoms does not in itself reveal what local action should be taken to correct the root problem. Discussion that does not result in action is fruitless talk. So while talk radio does well to get people engaged mentally, it widely tends to leave people hanging there without a hunger to take action, much less strategic action. Talk radio produces fat armchair quarterbacks, and angry ones at that. This is what I became.

So that's where our family hung for years—listening to political discussion (none of it being introduced to us from a Scriptural perspective) without knowing what action to take. Oddly enough, where we were taking action in our personal lives (my parents took full responsibility for our training and education instead of leaving it to the taxpayers who aren't minding the shop) it was easy to see the holes in talk radio where we saw the culture going to hell in a hand basket, and nary a caller would point out the obvious solution. That included us. See how deeply our inaction had settled?

We eventually started looking more closely into the Constitution, and through that we encountered David Barton, Michael Farris, Gary DeMar, and Douglas Wilson. DeMar's books led us to R.J. Rushdoony (whom I later learned my dad had read earlier in his 30s), Gary North, and Joel McDurmon shortly afterward. These authors and their understandings of Scripture have greatly advanced my religious journey which has produced this book. The best thing about these authors is their thorough focus on Scripture.

The Talmud (Jewish oral and written traditions), and Christian commentaries cover the subject of capital punishment, but they're spread across thousands of years and even more thousands of books. You're not going to go through all those. And even if you did, they would mostly only tell you how it was thought of and practiced historically, and maybe even why it was right a long time ago—not why it should be done today and how to begin moving Christian culture in that direction, which is the goal of this book.

Capital offenses are the weightiest of the weightier matters of the law that Christ warns about neglecting

(Matthew 23:23). This book is the largest collection of answers to the "why" of public execution, and it will conclude with currently the only collection of the "how-to for today." I hope the foundations presented here will prompt further discussion into practical implementation. Perhaps this book is looking too far into the future for God's people, but I would rather err on the side of looking too far forward rather than not far enough. I believe it's overdue for this position to have its own book.

Because I don't have all the answers on this subject, I hope to at least introduce you to the correct questions. No book is a final answer other than Scripture, which is where I hope to point you. You will find that many sections contain unanswered questions. (You have already encountered some.) Some people may be frustrated by these, perhaps thinking that I believe the answers to these questions are evident and expect readers to simply plug them in and carry on reading. That is not always the case. These questions are my own, and several important answers are not evident to me. And even then, I may still be wrong in the answers I reasonably think I do have. Some of these answers may be evident to you. I can't take you any further than I have gone myself. I can't give you answers that I don't have yet.

The best analogy I can offer is that this book is like a medical textbook; it will change and improve. Our understanding and skill in the law will change more so, and our resulting spirituality even more so.

CHAPTER 1

Willful Ignorance of Capital Offenses Within Christ's Body

I CONSIDERED PLACING STATISTICS here. And while statistics are important in creating a strategy, they are not useful in driving my point home: even if these personal anecdotes turn out to be incredibly uncommon (I won't debate the degree), that is no reason to have no justice system to deal with them. Houses don't catch fire often, yet there needs to be a system in place for how to put them out. You forget the ubiquity of fire hydrants on every street, but when they're needed,

it has made the difference of life and death to countless
people over decades. Having a godly system for dealing
with capital offenders is the most basic requirement for
any people. It's "STEP 1" for building society. Without
it, can you really have a cohesive city that stands firm in
the greatest adversity? A single member of the city can
dismantle it without some such system.

I was looking for a roommate. I had a Christian
brother refer me to another believer who was looking
for a place to rent. I'll call him Herman. I asked Herman
about his situation and found that he was seriously con-
sidering divorcing his wife. I told him that if he were
to divorce his wife and get remarried, that would be
adultery (Luke 16:18). I would consider that equal with
murder, and I wouldn't allow him to continue being a
roommate if he did that. He agreed, and he moved in as
a sub-lessee.

Several months later, I met his wife for the first time.
In our first conversation, she told me that Herman had
slept with my neighbor's wife recently while he had been
living in my house. I immediately went next door and
asked her if that was true. She said it was true. I went
back home and asked Herman if it was true. He wouldn't
answer. I said if it wasn't true, he could continue renting
from me. He immediately said he was moving out.

Soon after, I called his pastor at the gathering where
Herman played music regularly. I told him what the

neighbor's wife had told me as well as Herman's response when I confronted him about it. His response was, "Well, I can't live Herman's life for him." In other words, what was anyone supposed to do about it?

At two other assemblies nearby, both pastors had stepped down due to adultery and fornication. One has since returned to ministry where he was before. At the other assembly, a third man who was leading Bible studies once bragged to me about how long he put up with his "annoying" former wife before he divorced her and about how his new wife is so much better. He was gloating over his adultery after he just finished leading a Bible study.

I have personally heard three fellow believers blaspheme God's name since I started listening for it a few years ago. The one who is a pastor has not been removed. That pastor also laughed to me that his daughter called him a "Richard." He continued, "She said that it's because it's another name for a bad word. It was really clever. I was so proud of her." He was not joking. Speaking lightly of one's parents is a capital offense (Exodus 21:17).

I personally know two Christian women who have openly admitted to fornication multiple times. While not all fornication is a capital offense, it is for Israelites and daughters of priests (Deuteronomy 22:20-21, Leviticus 21:9), and all believers are priests and children of Abraham by faith (Revelation 1:5-6, Romans 2:26-29). These women still claim Christ's name (1 Corinthians 5:13).

I have heard other accounts of similarly serious offenses taking place over the years, divorce and remarriage being most common (Luke 16:18), along with false prophecy (Deuteronomy 18:20-22), children striking their parents and being gluttonous drunkards (Exodus 21:15, Deuteronomy 21:18-21), and cursing God in prayers to Him (Numbers 17:10).

Where is the mourning and repentance that we are called to as believers in 1 Corinthians 5:1-2? In 1 John 5:16-18, we are told not to pray for a brother who commits a sin that leads to death. Adultery is one such sin. It's one of the few that's still understood as being serious enough to be removed from the body, at least sometimes.

There are many more sins that are equally as bad that have been forgotten. Regardless, the penalty for murder and adultery is the same in Scripture. Why are these unrepentant people still considered part of their local bodies? The apostle Paul excommunicated men for blasphemy (1 Timothy 1:20), something that many believers today would consider to be rather inconsequential if they even recognized it happening at all.

Many of these offenses are so neglected there aren't even statistics on it. Where are the people stepping down from ministry due to having cursed their parents or struck them (Exodus 21:15, 1 Timothy 1:8), blasphemy, eating blood (Levititcus 17:10-14, Acts 15:29), or making a false prophecy in God's name? Where are these things seen as serious enough to be removed from the congregation by lawful means?

Even if these are not widespread problems (the degree is nebulous), isn't it best to have a plan for what to do before a catastrophe happens? It's best to think about the consequences for these matters before one is caught in an offense. God's design for capital offenses is intended to provide just such a teaching opportunity, yet even this warning of innocent by-standers is often neglected at best, and spoken of as unloving at worst.

We need to understand what God designed repentance to look like for a capital offense in the light of the law and what that means for believers today. It's highly uncomfortable by God's design, but refusing to understand the consequences of a capital offense will limit the grace these people seek from God. A sinner who has been forgiven little loves little (Luke 7:47).

CHAPTER 2

God's Authority and Heart in Public Execution

A MAN NAMED ANTONIN DEHAYS stole WWII dog tags from the National Museum of American History. He was fined tens of thousands of dollars and condemned to 364 days in prison. Was he punished because the museum didn't value the dog tags? Was it not because they were of great value to the museum and to the American culture? What message would it send if they didn't respond or simply gave a $20 fine? The punishment is proportional to the offense. I'm not defending the court's use of prison or its attitude that war relics are holy and sacred. But as an illustration, the punishment is supposed to fit the offense, and this court wanted to send a message that this was a serious offense and so met it with a serious punishment.

God says a life is worth a life. If we say that a life is worth less than a life, how can we say that we place a high value on life?

The goal of public stoning is righteousness and to spread fear of repeating deadly evil. In other words, the purpose is life. This is the undercurrent of the entire law. Even in the laws for making war, men have a prior responsibility to build houses, take wives, work the ground, and enjoy the fruit of the trees (Deuteronomy 20:5-7, 19-20). The great commission is at stake. We must disciple the nations. But how? Jesus tells us. The first part is to baptize them in the name of the Father, Son, and Holy Spirit. The second part is to teach them to observe all that He has commanded us (Matthew 28:18-20). This includes stoning. Jesus tells us that every part of the law, down to the smallest stroke and dot that make up individual letters of the law, is eternal (Matthew 5:17-20). Throughout the gospels, acts, epistles, and the prophetic work of Revelation, the validity of the law is assumed, specifically referenced, and upheld as good.

The letter of the law came through Moses, and the spirit of the law came through Christ. What does this mean? Throughout the Sermon on the Mount, Christ said not only is the law that adulterers should be put to death good, but the spirit of the law goes even further so that the act of even looking at a woman with lust is committing adultery in the heart. Hating a brother is also committing murder in the heart (Matthew 5:21-30). Christ never relaxed the law (Matthew 5:19); He tightened its requirements and gave new commandments (Matthew 19:8-9, John 13:34). The letter of the law is lax compared to the spirit of the law, and the spirit of the law is what gives life (2 Corinthians 3:6).

We see this attitude throughout the New Testament in examples of Paul using relatively obscure passages of the law to inform our conduct today. In 1 Corinthians 9:9, Paul writes that he does not instruct by human authority, but from the authority of the laws given to Moses. In 1 Timothy 5:18 and 1 Corinthians 9:9, Paul quotes Deuteronomy 25:4 to prove that he and Barnabas have the right to be paid for their work in teaching. The law there says not to muzzle the ox as it treads out the grain. Paul assumes that this law applies forever. Would it make sense to base a proof off of something that is no longer in effect? Paul is using the letter of the law, which is true and eternal, to show the spirit of the law, which is yet more true and eternal.

He does this again in Colossians 3:5. Just as the law says to put to death the evil person from among you, we are to put to death what is earthly in our hearts: sexual immorality, covetousness, idolatry, and other evils. What sense would it make to say this if people aren't supposed to put to death the evil person from among them? Wouldn't this contradict the point Paul makes?

Then in 1 Timothy 1:5-11, Paul writes a list of capital offenses, saying that the law is good to use lawfully, and in verse 11, he says that the goodness of the law is "in accordance with the glorious gospel." Later in 1 Timothy 5:19, Paul upholds and refers to the laws for witness requirements found in Deuteronomy 19:15. His assumption is that the law still applies in every detail. In verse 20, he cites that the basis for public rebuke for unrepentant sin among believers comes from the law in Exodus and Deuteronomy. He says to rebuke in public so that the rest may stand in fear. This principle is based on the fear that public stoning is also meant to instill (Exodus 23:1, Deuteronomy 13:11, 17:13, 19:20, 21:21).

Again in 1 Corinthians 5, Paul addresses the assembly at Corinth who are not mourning but arrogant that a man has his father's wife. This is forbidden in the law, even if it were his mother-in-law (Leviticus 20:11, Deuteronomy 27:23). And then Paul tells the body to hand the man over to Satan to destroy his flesh, that his soul may be saved, and thereby "purge the evil from among you." This is death penalty language. The phrase is only used in connection with capital punishment in

Deuteronomy 13:5, 17:7,12, 19:19, 21:21, 22:21-24, and 24:7. The Jews had made a Greek translation called the Septuagint from the original Hebrew, and Paul quotes this Greek translation word for word so that there's no mistake as to what he's referencing. If capital punishment according to the law is not something that God's people should even consider applying to themselves, why would Paul use a phrase only referring to the death penalty in the law as instruction for them when a man takes his father's wife?

And the most personal example for Paul is found in Acts 25. The Jews had had enough of his teaching about the Messiah and His fulfillment of the law. Due to their long rebellion to God, they had most of their authority to execute stripped away from them by Rome for generations. They wished that Paul were dead, so they charge him by Jewish and Roman law of being guilty of death, anything they can do to get Festus the procurator to execute him by Roman authority. In verse 8, Paul says that there is nothing to their charges of violating Jewish law, and that if there were, he would not seek to escape death in verses 10-11. If Paul were ever going to make the case that capital offenses did not deserve death at the hands of the people, wouldn't it have been then? Not only does he not make this case, but also he says if there is merit to the accusations, he agreed that he should die! Contrast this with Acts 9:23-25 where Paul succeeded in escaping

the Jews who plotted to kill him. So he simultaneously upholds the goodness and validity of the law while saying by
his actions that there was no merit to their accusations.

Now let's move to two examples of Jesus directly. The
first is found in Luke 19:1-10 with Zacchaeus. Zacchaeus
was a tax collector and had sinned greatly by collecting
much more in taxes than he was authorized to do (Luke
3:13). Zacchaeus knew the law of restitution for stealing,
and so he knew the appropriate action to take to bear
the fruits of repentance. He offered fourfold and fivefold
restitution as found in Exodus 22:1, which King David
also condemned himself with in 2 Samuel 12:1-7. These
are no random amounts that Zacchaeus is offering. He
offers four times the extra amounts he had collected from
those he had defrauded. Where did Zacchaeus come up
with this amount?

There are three penalty levels for theft:

1. A repentant thief who returns the stolen proper-
    ty on the day he realizes his guilt must restore the
    property and pay an additional fifth and offer a
    ram or equivalent as a sacrifice (Leviticus 6:1-7).
2. A thief who is caught with the stolen property
    must restore double the property (Exodus 22:4, 7).
3. A thief who steals property and either sells or
    destroys what was stolen must pay a fivefold or
    fourfold penalty (Exodus 22:1).

Jesus doesn't condemn Zacchaeus for wanting to repent by obeying the laws for restitution. He doesn't tell Zacchaeus, "A day is coming and is now here where you won't have to bow down in the letter of the law." He actually tells Zacchaeus that salvation has come to his house as evidenced by his faithful obedience to the law. This is a play on words, because Jesus's name in Hebrew is "Yeshua," which means "the LORD saves." It was obviously literally true since Jesus is salvation for all who believe; He was physically come to Zacchaeus's house. But it was also true spiritually as evidenced by the fruit of Zacchaeus's repentance. We have no other record of Jesus saying this to anyone.

Since Zacchaeus was repentant in this matter, even though he was guilty of the third level of theft (profiting from it), a ram was to be sacrificed for him as in the first level. Jesus, who was standing in front of him that moment, was that ram or equivalent to be sacrificed.

And finally Jesus's own opinion of stoning is shown in Mark 7:5-13. The Pharisees bring up a point of dissension with Jesus because his disciples don't follow the traditions of the elders. Jesus condemns them for their traditions because not only do they refuse to execute children who revile their parents, the Pharisees encourage children in their reviling with a tradition that they set above God's law. So Jesus condemns the Pharisees for encouraging children to commit a capital offense instead of stoning them to death for it.

Yet what nation won't be destroyed by such laws? The only reason societies continue to live is because God is merciful. This does not mean disobedience is acceptable. We know that obedience in the first place is better than disobedience first and then being granted mercy later (1 Samuel 15:22, Hosea 6:6). One day, death will die, and there will no longer be any need for mercy because there will no longer be any sin. Obedience will remain, and it is better than mercy, which is why God gives mercy (which has less value) in exchange for our obedience (which has more value). Obedience is doing the right thing the first time. Mercy is offering to obey on someone else's behalf after he has disobeyed. The former is of higher value.

When King David committed adultery with Bathsheba against Uriah and then killed Uriah with the sword, God condemned David's illegitimate son to death to preserve David's life (2 Samuel 12:13-14). David wished that he had obeyed from the start. The child's death was God's mercy to David, but David's obedience would have been better.

So if we as believers fail to practice justice, we are a bad witness for Christ. The neglect of discussing and practicing these laws are hurting God's people and preventing us from growing by attracting outsiders by our fruit of the spirit (Deuteronomy 4:5-8, Galatians 5:22-23).

The righteousness we are to exemplify is like a person's health. A healthy person seeks out what's best for him to eat and do to take care of his body. But if he does something foolish and breaks his leg, a good diet isn't going to set a broken limb or mend a torn ligament. If left unattended long enough, amputation may even be necessary. Likewise, if there's a growing tumor that's threatening to block someone's airways, a knife and some cutting must be done to ultimately save the rest of his body (Matthew 5:29, 18:9).

Christian community, like any community, is based on a system of blessings and curses which exist on a spectrum. In a family, certain privileges are obtained by trust and heightened accountability. This trust carries penalties for breaking faith in proportion to the weight of trust a task requires. Without greater consequences for disobedience, like priests in the temple (compare Exodus 22:16 and Leviticus 21:9), there can be no access granted for service. For example: a large business wouldn't trust an unknown pedestrian from the street to be the new executive decision-maker. If he is given actual control, he must be fully aware of the serious consequences of failure or breaking faith. Otherwise, there is too much risk of damage if he becomes untrustworthy.

Dealing with capital offenses is the most basic tenet of any nation. If a nation has no will to remove murderers and other capital offenders from all contact with its people, it will eventually collapse or be destroyed. The goal is honoring God which results in a healthy nation, long life, and prosperity (Deuteronomy 28:1-14).

In the same way, God's design for life and growth must include rewards for obedient living, and it must include punishment for disobedient living, including death so that further damage to others is avoided (see Deuteronomy 28's blessings and cursings). To neglect a "whole view" (positive and negative aspects) of righteousness is like saying: "All a person will ever need to be healthy is a good diet and exercise, no matter if it's obesity or a life-threatening tumor."

All nations realize that certain actions cannot be allowed to any extent without undermining the foundation of human life. In our current day, many nations we find ourselves in agree with God on a few key issues when it relates to life-and-death matters. Some of these are murder, negligent killing, repeated drunkenness and rebellion against authority, kidnapping people, maybe the rape of a married woman, adultery and male homosexual acts in some parts of the world, and that's about it. While these are good, there are many more capital offenses that God warns us about, many of which are rampant among those who bear God's name.

In Texas where I was born and raised (not to conflate any earthly nation with God's nation), there have been about 700 murder convictions and 576 murder executions since 1982 (as of 2022). To put that in perspective, there have been over 63,000 murders reported (by participating jurisdictions) in that same time period in Texas. So assuming that there are no additional murders in the jurisdictions that don't report, let's assume that every murderer killed 3 people; that's 21,000 murderers. Assuming every 20th murderer is convicted and executed; that's 1,050 executions required for murderers alone. That's almost double the amount we see, and these assumptions are absurdly low, and the average number killed by each murderer is absurdly high.

This does not include anything else in the list of capital offenses that will be outlined in chapter 4, many of which even many Christians couldn't care less about. I think it is a safe bet to say that there are many more children who curse their parents than there are murders committed, and with more witnesses too. This is not a society that values life. We must do better, and God's people must lead the way.

CHAPTER 3

Why Prison as Punishment Is Unjustified

THERE WAS A FAMILY IN OUR CON-
gregation who had a son that spent over a year in a federal prison for stealing cars and selling them across state lines. After he was released, an affected party tracked him down and sued him for compensation for the cars. If he went to prison to pay for his offense and the authorities deemed it finished, how is it allowable for someone to continue to seek compensation in the courts? What did his time spent in prison actually pay for? In this case, he

is a felon for life even after "serving his time." And yet "serving time" cost the people he stole from by way of a delay of justice (over a year of waiting for him to be released), and by paying taxes to keep the prison in operation. Putting him in prison hurt his victims. They would have been best served if he were required to provide immediate fourfold or fivefold restitution (Exodus 22:1).

In Matthew 5:25-26 and Luke 12:58-59, Jesus instructs us to come to terms quickly with our accusers on the way to court, lest we be put in prison. He tells us that we will never escape until we have paid the last penny. This is a statement of fact rather than a reason why we may ignore God's law for what to do with a lawbreaker. The pattern Scripture lays out is that even if we rebel and neglect to obey God, God will make us captives (Deuteronomy 28:15-68). Prison and captivity is the end of the road. God uses wicked nations to judge His people when they rebel. This is not to cast a positive light on the wicked nations or their use of prison, but to give us a taste of our wickedness. The main point Jesus makes is about how repentance and reconciliation must be sought before judgment is made against us. It will be easier for us that way to settle out of court. I believe He used this illustration in particular because His audience was under Roman occupation which did practice prison. This does not mean Israel (or anyone else) is following God's will in doing so.

Three types of prison in Scripture

We find prison used in two cases where an offender was placed under guard until God's will was made clear for punishment. A man blasphemes in Leviticus 24:10-16, and a man breaks the sabbath in Numbers 15:32-36. Both of these are capital offenses. Notice how in each case where the men were placed under guard or custody, it was because God had not yet made it clear what should be done with them. It's fair to call this jail or prison, and that was because the people had not been given the law yet regarding these men. Also, being in custody was not the punishment; it was to hold them until God's word had been made clear.

The second way Scripture refers to prison/jail/being placed under guard is when Israel locked up prophets it despised. If God's people had prison or jail buildings as common practice, we are nowhere told. There are only three people mentioned in Scripture whom Israel put in prison as punishment. All were prophets suffering at the unjust rulings of kings and priests. The first account is in 2 Chronicles 16:1-10 when Asa king of Judah was angered by a rebuke that the prophet Hanani gave him regarding an alliance with Ben-hadad king of Syria. The second is in the case of Micaiah the prophet in 1 Kings 22:13-28 and the parallel passage in 2 Chronicles 18:12-27. King Ahab also didn't like what the prophet was telling him. The last account of Hebrew imprisonment is Jeremiah. He was first beaten and put into the stocks in the temple gate by Pashhur the priest (Jeremiah 20:1-23), then he was in the court of the guard in the king's palace in Judah (32:2-3), then he was placed in the house of Jonathan the secretary which had been turned into a prison with dungeon cells (37:15-16), then he went back to the court of the guard (37:21), then he was thrown into a cistern with no water (38:6), then they lifted him out and put him back in the court of the guard (38:13) until he was released by order of Nebuchadnezzar (39:11-14).

Asa, Ahab, and Zedekiah didn't like the judgments that Hanani, Micaiah, and Jeremiah foretold against them, and they were too afraid to kill prophets directly. All three kings saw the option of imprisonment as a suitable compromise. This compromise is not an option, for if a prophet is a false prophet, the penalty is death (Deuteronomy 18:20), and if the prophet is truthful, he should be heard, not isolated to silence him. We can see by how many times Jeremiah was shuffled around that there was no regular system in place in Israel for where to put someone whom the king wanted silenced but not killed.

And finally, the third kind of use of prison in Scripture is when the nations practice imprisonment. The earliest currently known uses of prison were in ancient Egypt and Mesopotamia. Scripture's first reference to prison is in Genesis 39:20. Joseph is falsely accused by Potiphar's wife of violating her. This charge by a single witness is sustained by the Egyptian authorities (Deuteronomy 19:15). Moreover, it is a malicious accusation (Deuteronomy 19:18-19). Joseph is placed in a "bet ha-sohar" (round house) where men are bound and held for long periods of time after being accused and condemned (Genesis 40:1-4). In 2 Kings 25:27-30 and the parallel passage in Jeremiah 52:31-34, Jehoiachin king of Judah was held prisoner by Evil-merodach king of Babylon after Judah had been taken captive there. This use of prison is an example of God using a crooked stick to beat another crooked stick straight. The pagan kingdoms behaved lawlessly in their conquering of Judah as God's judgment for Judah's idolatry. This is not to put Babylonian rulers in a positive light (Jeremiah 25:11-14) but to punish Judah for its rebellion. Later in Ezra 7:26, when Artaxerxes I (a subsequent Persian king) is sending Ezra back to Jerusalem, he grants and encourages Ezra in his authority to punish the disobedient. He lists imprisonment as one of the possible punishments that Ezra may impose. Should this be taken as a new option for Jews to practice based on a Persian king's exhortation? Why should Artaxerxes be allowed to add laws? This may simply be a display of ignorance of Moses on his part.

Other examples include John the Baptist being put in prison by Roman authority in Matthew 14:1-12, Mark 6:14-29, Luke 3:18-20 and 9:7-9, the apostles being arrested in Acts 5:17-26, Saul persecuting the body by throwing members in prison in Acts 8:3; 22:4, 19; 26:10, Peter being imprisoned by Herod in Acts 12:1-17, and Paul and Silas being imprisoned by the owner of a fortune-teller in Acts 16:19-40.

Holding someone under guard today as the punishment itself is rejecting God in two ways:

1. It is acting as if God has not yet made it clear what to do with offenders.

2. It rejects what God has now clearly said to do with a given offender.

God's design is to teach the public how to avoid wrongdoing before it occurs. Prison appears to be a solution, but it's only temporary because it doesn't get to the heart of the problem. A judicial system that is designed to prick hearts is much more involved to implement, but in the long term, it's a much easier path. As the saying goes, "Give a man a fish, and you feed him for a day; teach a man to fish, and you feed him for a lifetime." For a fisherman, catching a fish to give away takes less time than teaching someone else how to catch his own fish from scratch. But if you want to feed millions, you have to teach others to fish. People in prison are the ones who need to be taught.

Prisons or even holding places are not commanded in Scripture. Scripture lays out systems of restitution and atonement. So when nations use prison in a way

that causes anyone harm, it's because it sees no redemp-
tive path forward otherwise. So at the very least, prison
must be seen as a tradition. It's either an allowable tradition for those awaiting judgment, or it's a sinful tradition used to nullify God's commands. Of course, doing
something absent from Scripture is not necessarily a
violation of a commandment. Watching TV or using a
phone is not necessarily wrong. What would be wrong
is ignoring clear commands. Prison and jail ignore what
is supposed to be done with capital offenders, and additionally, holding someone as punishment itself or as
collateral for payment violates a prohibition.

"No one shall take a mill or an upper millstone
in pledge, for that would be taking a life in pledge"
(Deuteronomy 24:6). The word for "pledge" is "chabal"
which means to bind or destroy. In context, it carries the
idea of holding something as collateral or for ransom,
either duly or in an oppressive way. A millstone is a tool
for grinding grain to make bread. So to take someone's
tools that he needs to use in order to eat is prohibited.
That would be binding or effectively destroying that person's life. And if taking someone's means of working to
eat is the same as binding someone's life itself, how much
more does it prohibit binding someone's life directly, his
own body! Taking a life in pledge is prohibited.

Why is it important that someone's tools for work
or life not be bound? Because it makes it unnecessarily

difficult for the person to work to repay the debt (if indeed it can be paid for this way). This is God's standard for how offenses are to be punished: whatever is taken, the same is to be paid back by service or life. The punishment is designed to teach the people the value of what was stolen (Ephesians 4:28). And for a capital offense, prison delays justice, delays payment. God's justice is designed to teach people the value of life. Justice delayed will encourage men to do more evil (Ecclesiastes 8:11).

In the example of Joseph, Scripture doesn't specify whether his imprisonment was intended to be the punishment itself, or if he was simply awaiting the actual penalty. He and others with him simply spent years in bondage. Exodus 21:19 requires compensation when someone injures a person that causes loss of work. So holding someone to await punishment must at a minimum require compensation for his time if he is released without any other penalty. For Joseph, God had a purpose for his imprisonment and used it to ultimately save His people from starvation. God often miraculously brings good out of mankind's evil. Just as the Jews were not justified in crucifying Jesus, Joseph's brothers were not justified in unlawfully selling him into slavery (Exodus 21:6). Potiphar's wife maliciously reported Joseph to her husband for adultery when she was actually the one attempting to commit adultery. Yet God brings good from all these situations. Does God then hold these people guiltless? Jerusalem was destroyed for rejecting and crucifying Jesus, and Egypt was judged for its wickedness also. This is no excuse for wickedness in someone's heart. And it's not necessarily a justification for using prison.

People criticize God's law as archaic and obsolete. Yet they adopt a system of imprisonment practiced by the ancient Egyptians. If we agree with parts of Egyptian practice, the Egyptians also practiced stoning (Exodus 8:25-27). Why only adopt part of the Egyptian morality when Scripture endorses stoning and precludes and prohibits prison? This is an outright rejection of God's commandments. One requirement is ignored, and a tradition is adopted to try to compensate. The Pharisees were skilled at this (Mark 7:8-9). We should not wish to be like them. If we're going to agree with Egyptian practice in part, why not consider their other practices for inspiration? I think most would agree that Egypt is not and should not be our standard. So what should be? Why are prisons a good idea and stoning a bad idea? If someone is permitted to discount God's law because it is "old" or "barbaric," then prison may also be discounted by the same token. One method or another will fill the void to deal with offenders, whether it's God's law or man-made tradition.

Problems in the world's courts

1. The current legal system is slow. The average felony case takes 256 days just to get to disposition, not resolution.[1] The public has not been taught God's law by His body of people (which is our primary duty). This results in a large amount of charges and disputes which could be avoided by effective teaching and discipling on matters of law. The body of Christ has been largely silent and willfully avoided political discussion. Politics are simply the practical moral issues of the day. Therefore Christ's body in general has decided that if it's a moral topic that the culture is hungry to discuss, it does not address it as a matter of policy. Additionally, not only does the body do a relatively poor job about judging all matters within itself, it often rejects this as a responsibility.

2. The current legal system is expensive: according to Self Defense Fund, the average cost for a trial where the death penalty is on the table is $1,300,000. If the death penalty is not on the table, $600,000. This does not include the costs of jail time, prison expenses, appeals, or the cost

1. Brian J. Ostrom, et al., "Timely Justice in Criminal Cases: What the Data Tells Us" (Williamsburg, VA: National Center for State Courts, 2020). Available online at https://www.ncsc.org/__data/assets/pdf_file/0019/53218/Timely-Justice -in-Criminal-Cases-What-the-Data-Tells-Us.pdf

for the prosecution. This only includes defense costs. A current "cheap, open-shut" case would cost around $25,000.

3.   The current legal system is unjust: there are many traditions that allow or mandate injustice to be practiced. This includes things like entering a plea, trial by jury, reducing sentencing, and incarceration.

4.   The current legal system is difficult to improve: the system of man-made traditions (often called "laws") governing each jurisdiction is tied up in the city, county, state, and federal "laws" and case "law." (I use quotes for "law" because any law in addition to God's law is simply tradition or statute (Psalm 94:20). Changing these traditions takes time, money, deals, and bribes, not to mention public favor.

5.   Only a select few can enforce the law: this is a difficult idea to overcome. Every person should be allowed to arrest and compel anyone to appear before a judge to face accusation directly. In an upstanding city where the people have a firm grasp on this practice, that city won't need to pay people to carry this out. But if anyone can arrest anyone, wouldn't that enable a lot of injustice to

occur? Yes, which is why there is an equal standard for anyone who arrests another. If the arrest
is false, whoever brought the charge and brought
about the arrest must suffer the penalty for the
accusation he falsely brought. This would nullify the American tradition of "probable cause."
False charges would be rarely brought due to the
risk of punishment associated with false charges.
God's standard requires eyewitnesses, not merely
physical evidence. Physical evidence is there to
validate eyewitness testimony, not stand in place
of it. This would also eliminate number 6.

6. Qualified immunity can grant an officer protection
    from legal consequences when he breaks the law:
    if a court deems that an officer reasonably broke
    the law, he can be held harmless. This concept is
    unlawful, and it encourages unlawful actions from
    officials. The consequences of police being granted
    qualified immunity is easily seen in higher depres-
    sion and suicide rates among law officers. They
    can't escape the guilt of a system that allows them
    to falsely or baselessly arrest or accuse people
    with little to no personal risk of facing the conse-
    quences for a false arrest or accusation. God's law
    only speaks of correct accusations and malicious

accusations. It is silent on the concept of dropping charges without consequence to the accuser.

There are many more problems such as appeal by defendant, prison sentences, confession standards and witness requirements, separation of civil and criminal courts, and many others. The younger you are, the more strongly I would recommend that you forget everything you know about your local system of courts and judges and start from scratch with Scripture.

CHAPTER 4

God's Ideal

WHILE THE FOLLOWING CHART MAY
seem out of place and not strictly within the subject of
capital offenses, it is foundational to understanding how
to deal with capital offenses. The laws for capital offenses plug into this chart.

I can't overstate the importance of the underlying
Scriptures. I could spend a great amount of time critiqu-
ing and picking contemporary legal systems apart. While
I will provide some limited examples of error, examples
of error pale in comparison to knowing the ideal. When
2+2=4 is known for certain, all the wrong answers don't
have to be explained as to why they are wrong. God's
commandments are that certain answer.

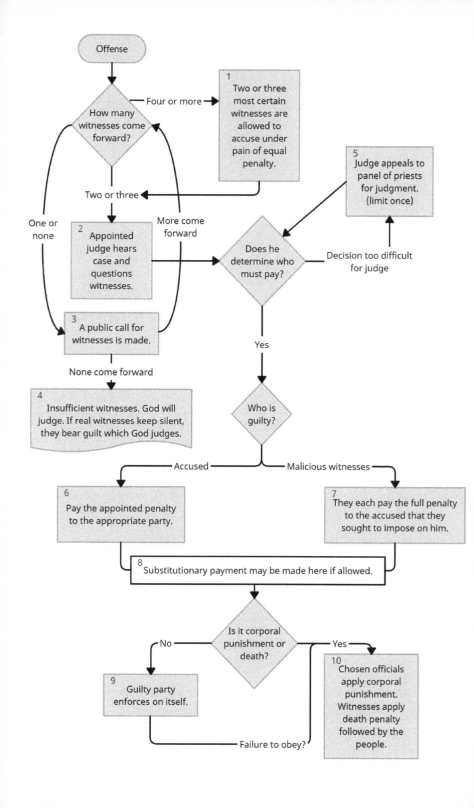

Offense

How many witnesses come forward?

Four or more → 1. Two or three most certain witnesses are allowed to accuse under pain of equal penalty.

Two or three

One or none

More come forward

2. Appointed judge hears case and questions witnesses.

3. A public call for witnesses is made.

None come forward

4. Insufficient witnesses. God will judge. If real witnesses keep silent, they bear guilt which God judges.

Does he determine who must pay?

Decision too difficult for judge

5. Judge appeals to panel of priests for judgment. (limit once)

Yes

Who is guilty?

Accused — Malicious witnesses

6. Pay the appointed penalty to the appropriate party.

7. They each pay the full penalty to the accused that they sought to impose on him.

8. Substitutionary payment may be made here if allowed.

Is it corporal punishment or death?

No — Yes

9. Guilty party enforces on itself.

Failure to obey?

10. Chosen officials apply corporal punishment. Witnesses apply death penalty followed by the people.

1. Deuteronomy 17:6, 19:15, Matthew 18:16-20, John 8:17-18, 1 Corinthians 14:27-29, 2 Corinthians 13:1, 1 Timothy 5:19, Hebrews 10:28, 1 John 5:7-9, Revelation 11:3

2. Deuteronomy 16:18, 17:9, 19:18

3. Leviticus 5:1, Deuteronomy 17:4, 21:1

4. Deuteronomy 19:15, Leviticus 5:1, 1 Timothy 5:19

5. Deuteronomy 17:8-13, 19:17, 21:5, Mark 14:53, John 18:19-24

6. Exodus 21:22, 22:1-31, Deuteronomy 17:9, 19:17

7. Deuteronomy 19:16-21

8. Exodus 21:30, Numbers 35:33

9. Deuteronomy 17:12-13

10. Deuteronomy 13:9-11, 21:21, 25:1-3, 1 Corinthians 5:13, 2 Corinthians 11:24

God's obstacles to stoning

If any of these situations occur, the accused may still be guilty, but God prohibits the people from putting the accused to death:

1. Not enough witnesses: a confession alone or a single witness is not a sufficient number of witnesses. Two or three must establish a charge. No more, no less (Deuteronomy 17:6, 19:5).

2. False witnesses: if malicious witnesses are found, they are punished to match the charges they brought (Deuteronomy 19:18-19).

3. Witnesses unwilling to cast the first stones: their testimonies are not acceptable, and the accusation can't be made (Deuteronomy 13:9, 17:7).

4. Public inserts itself to block stoning: if someone is guilty despite this, God brings the consequences on all the people. If the person was innocent, God will bless the people and hold the witnesses and judge responsible (Leviticus 20:1-2, 1 Samuel 14:24-48, Matthew 27:25).

God's ideal design

All sin is worthy of death. For some sins, with the required witnesses, God commands us to execute offenders. This following foldout is an exhaustive list of every capital offense in the law, organized by category. These laws are like a living organism with connections and parallels everywhere. I am not settled or satisfied with this presentation. Consider this a time-saving resource for you to study and expand on in your own further study. Scan the QR code to the right or visit voluntarytheocracy.org/stoning.

Abridged list of accounts related to the death penalty, proper and improper

1. Moses worries about the Egyptians stoning them (Exodus 8:26)

2. Israel wants to stone Moses (Exodus 17)

3. Man who blasphemed (Leviticus 24:11-23)

4. Israel says to stone Moses after Moses tells them to take the spied-out land (Numbers 13:35-14:10)

5. Man who broke the sabbath (Numbers 15:32-36)

6. Achan (Joshua 7)

7. Jabesh-gilead broke its oath to come up to the LORD in Mizpah (Judges 21:5-11)

8. Saul commanding the execution of his son Jonathan when Jonathan ate honey contrary to Saul's vow (1 Samuel 14:24-48)

9. David ordering the killing of the man who lies about having killed Saul (2 Samuel 1:1-16)

10. Slaughter of innocent Ish-bosheth (2 Samuel 4:5-12)

11. Death of Uzzah (2 Samuel 6:1-7, 1 Chronicles 13:9-12)

12. The death of of Shimei (2 Samuel 16:5; 19:16-23, 1 Kings 2:8-9, 36-46)

13. Benaiah executes Joab for Solomon (1 Kings 2:5-6, 28-34)

14. Benaiah executes Adonijah for Solomon (1 Kings 2:13-25)

15. Naboth's vineyard (1 Kings 21:2-15)

16. Jehoshaphat exterminates male cult prostitutes (1 Kings 22:43-46)

17. Israel stones H/Adoram the slave taskmaster under Rehoboam (1 Kings 12:18, 2 Chronicles 10:18)

18. King Amaziah executes the men who killed his father the king (2 Kings 14:5-6)

19. Joash orders the stoning of Zechariah and is himself assassinated (2 Chronicles 24:17-25)

20. Parable of the tenants (Matthew 21:33-41, Mark 12:1-9)

21. Jesus's trial (Matthew 27, Mark 14:53-15:20, Luke 22:66-23:25, John 18:28-19:16)

22. *Woman caught in adultery (John 7:53-8:11) *(text has dubious authenticity)

23. Pharisees pick up stones to stone Jesus (John 8:58-59, 10:30-33)

24. The stoning of Stephen (Acts 7:54-60)

25. Gentiles, Jews, and rulers attempt to stone the apostles (Acts 14:3-7)

26. The stoning of Paul (Acts 14:19-20)

Avenger of blood

Numbers 35, Deuteronomy 19:1-13, and Joshua 20 command a certain protection for a man who unintentionally kills another. God appointed six of the forty-eight cities given to the Levites as cities of refuge (Kedesh in Galilee, Shechem, Kiriath-arba that is Hebron, Bezer, Ramoth in Gilead, and Golan in Bashan). Anyone who deliberately killed a person with a tool of iron, wood, stone, or by any other means was a murderer, and the cities of refuge offered no protection. It was only a protection for accidental or unintentional manslaughter.

For the manslayer who was not a murderer, he could flee to one of the cities, and the avenger of blood could not do anything to him as long as he was within one of these cities. If the avenger of blood found the manslayer outside the city for any reason, and assuming there were sufficient witnesses of the manslaughter, he was authorized to kill him. This was to remain in effect until the high priest died, and then the manslayer could return and was given his former status of innocence. Christ is the high priest who has died once for all, and we take refuge in Him, looking forward to the heavenly Jerusalem that is to come. All who are found in Christ died with Him, and the avenger of blood no longer has claim over them. No one should be put to death for accidental manslaughter anymore, because Christ, the final high priest, has died. However, this only applies to accidental manslaughter, not any other type of offense, not even negligent manslaughter, as the avenger of blood only applied for a single kind of offense.

Focusing on the term "avenger of blood," the word translated "avenger" is not the same as in verses where God says, "Vengeance is mine, and recompense" (Deuteronomy 32:35a). The word translated as "vengeance" there is "nakam," and is translated as "vengeance" and never anything but "vengeance." Yet in all the passages about the cities of refuge, the word translated as "avenger" in "avenger of blood" is actually the word translated as "kinsman," "redeemer," or "buy back" in every other place where it appears in Scripture. The word is "gaal," and it is the same word used in Ruth to describe Boaz, for he redeemed or bought back Ruth in marriage as a close relative to Ruth's deceased father. Nowhere outside of this manslayer situation is "gaal" rendered as "avenger."

"Gaal" is used when God buys back Israel from Egyptian slavery (Exodus 6:6) or when someone redeems land or redeems a brother who is a slave in the land by purchasing his freedom (Leviticus 25:25-55). Jeremiah 50:34 speaks of the "gaal" (the redeemer, who is the LORD) giving rest to the land by pleading the cause of the oppressed. Rest for the land is achieved by cleansing the pollution that murder produces. Payment for murder is not acceptable except by the one who shed the blood

(Numbers 35:31-34). Without the murderer being put to death, the land will remain polluted.

So the "avenger of blood" is more consistently translated or understood as "blood redeemer" or "buyer of blood." How can Scripture consider putting a murderer to death a "redemption," purchase, or restoring to a state of freedom? What good would it do to "gaal" (buy) the blood of a dead man? Would buying it bring him back to life? The purpose of redeeming blood is to cleanse the land. The blood of Abel cried out to God from the ground after Cain had murdered him (Genesis 4:10). The redeemer of blood is representing God and acting on His behalf. Putting a murderer to death is repaying God what is His due. God makes a claim on the blood of one who sheds blood. A life is worth a life. Blood is worth blood. If we withhold payment or deny that it is required, the polluted land will vomit us out (Leviticus 18:24-30). We reap what we sow. If we sow pollution to the land (innocent blood), we will reap pollution in our bodies, for we are made from the dust of the earth (Genesis 3:19).

But didn't Christ redeem manslayers? Yes! So does that mean a murderer should no longer wish to pay for the wrong he has done? Would someone bring up the same objection for a thief? Let's say a thief has stolen $500. Would a repentant thief argue that Christ died to pay for his theft, so now he doesn't have to restore the money when asked? This is not in the spirit of redemption.

Only someone intent on reviling Christ's sacrifice would use it as a reason to refuse to right his wrongdoing, for he has no evidence of the law being written on his heart. This is not consistent action for someone who has been freed from sin, but rather of someone using freedom in Christ as a cover-up for evil (1 Peter 2:16).

Phinehas the priest

In Numbers 25:1-13, God sent a plague that killed 24,000 Israelites because they were intermarrying with the Moabites and other peoples who caused them to turn to idolatry. As a result, God commanded Moses to hang the chiefs of the people in the sun. After this commandment, Phinehas the priest saw someone bringing a Midianite woman to his family in the midst of the plague. Phinehas put a spear through Zimri son of Salu and Cozbi daughter of Zur for their intermarrying, and the plague immediately stopped. In verse 13, it says that Phinehas's act of putting them to death was an atonement for Israel. The death penalty properly applied is not a separate concept from atonement or contrary to it; it is in harmony with it.

David writes of Phinehas,

> "Then they yoked themselves to the Baal of Peor,
> and ate sacrifices offered to the dead;
> they provoked the Lord to anger with their deeds,

and a plague broke out among them.

Then Phinehas stood up and intervened,

and the plague was stayed.

And that was counted to him as righteousness

from generation to generation forever" (Psalm
   106:28-31).

(This Phinehas is not to be confused with another priest named Phinehas who was the wicked son of Eli.)

God describes the death penalty in this case as "kaphar" (redemption, covering, propitiation). If anyone opposes the death penalty, he opposes God's design for redemption. The same word "kaphar" is used in Isaiah 6:7 when the angel touched Isaiah's lips with the burning coal. If anyone rejects the letter of the law, that is, the earthly things like the death penalty, how will he accept the spirit of the law, that is, the heavenly things like redemption (John 3:12)?

Did God really say?

The first temptation of Satan in the garden of Eden consisted of throwing doubt on God's commandment. Because of this tendency of mankind to readily entertain reasons why we don't need to obey certain laws of God, I believe it is a much safer and more consistent method to assume that all commandments from God are eternal and apply forever. There has been a change in the law with the change in the priesthood (Hebrews 7:12). A change does not mean a relaxing (Matthew 5:19) or an abrogation or nullification (Matthew 5:17). On the contrary, the word translated here as "change" ("metathesis") is used two other times in the New Testament: Hebrews 11:5 and 12:27. In both of these other uses, it refers to something ascending to heaven, being made then heavenly and unshakable. Every law is eternal. The Levitical priesthood and law were incomplete (Hebrews 7:11). Christ has completed them both. When something is completed, it does not vanish; it is more present than it was previously. Hebrews 8:13 speaks of the old covenant passing away because the new has come. What is the new covenant? It consists of the law being placed in our hearts rather than being written on stone (verse 10). Now they are written on flesh. The old covenant was the law broken. The new covenant is the law obeyed.

When unbelievers blaspheme by accusing our God of being evil, I have heard many believers attempt to apologize for God and explain why God doesn't actually intend for us to heed large chunks of Exodus, Leviticus, Numbers, and Deuteronomy, foremost among these laws are usually slavery or stoning. Believers fear looking archaic and backwards, and this emboldens the unbelievers. I agree with many unbelievers and atheists that these inconsistencies between our own book and our hearts are glaring problems, and anyone who decides to ignore them is ignorant, deceived, or has a rebellious heart.

CHAPTER 5

Benefits and Drawbacks Today

What is the good fruit of lawful public stoning?

1. **It scares the public away from evil thereby making itself less necessary and less likely to be needed every time it is carried out.**

Scripture frequently repeats the primary purpose of stoning: that all the people may hear and fear and never do such a thing among you again (Deuteronomy 13:11,

17:13, 19:20, 21:21). Like all punishments in Scripture, the goal is to teach people the consequences for wrongdoing. This is just as how biblically lawful slavery is designed to teach men to work instead of steal so that all men may be free (Ephesians 4:28). Just as lawful slavery is designed to make all men free, so public stoning is designed to make itself more unnecessary. When people are afraid to do evil because of having taken part in a violent execution, there will be less cause to stone someone else. This is meant to work in conjunction with desirable and righteous conduct being widely taught and culturally expected of everyone as well.

One of the first things you teach children about electricity is not to stick anything in an outlet. This is very important yet very simple. If a young boy is moments away from a dangerous electrocution, who wouldn't swat his hand away? Is this not done out of love? Electricity must be kept nearby and in its proper place to be enjoyed and simultaneously avoid injury. The same is true for weapons, fire, sex, our words, and every other potentially deadly tool. If someone does something wrong, and someone dies as a consequence, we naturally want to know what happened; we *should* know what happened. This helps us learn what steps to avoid. To make light of these important details, to ignore them, or to keep them secret, this is a disservice to everyone around. That would prevent them from learning from others' mistakes. By implication, it's wishing that the same consequences might happen to someone else for lack of knowledge. This is why stoning must be done in public. The sins leading up to it must be remembered with fear.

There are many other fruits that are products of this main fruit. Greater trust could be given to strangers and expected from strangers, not to mention known people in a city. Parents would fear God in raising their children or risk their efforts in child-rearing being put to a sudden end.

The most recent person to be executed by firing squad in the US was Ronnie Lee Gardner in 2010. In a VICE news story on HBO, Sheryl Worsley, a reporter who witnessed the execution, said, "The execution felt violent. It felt jarring, but at the same time it felt clinical, and professional, and clean. And I know that sounds like an oxymoron, but it truly felt sterile." The report goes on to say that three out of nine prisoners on death row in Utah prefer death by firing squad to lethal injection (source: YouTube "Should Firing Squads Replace Lethal Injections? (HBO)"). A firing squad is not stoning, but it's closer than lethal injection in many regards. It's supposed to involve public action to help the people remember and be afraid of doing evil too. Little metal rocks were used, but not by the witnesses in the case.

Mankind was created with a conscience, a knowledge of right and wrong. When someone deserves death and continues living, it's a great cause for pain. David wrote many psalms asking God why He allows the wicked to continue in their sin. Many people today struggle with similar thoughts, and they don't know the answer that David knew. A lack of justice emboldens people to do more evil. David found great comfort in God's everlasting justice because he knew it will always come. Slow justice encourages people to do more evil (Ecclesiastes 8:11-13). God's design is for justice to be swift to discourage evildoers.

2. False witnesses being required to suffer the sought penalty of their charge strongly discourages bearing false witness.

Making malicious or baseless accusations of capital offenses such as blasphemy, kidnapping, or adultery would be made very rare due to the risk of death involved for the accusers. False accusations of a capital offense are punished with death in a Biblical system of law (Deuteronomy 19:16-20). And if the accusation is true, the accusers must personally cast the first stones. This is not a responsibility that can be handed over to someone else. This is how sure such an accusation must be.

3. The witnesses and then the community are the means of execution, which is meant to prevent abuses by authorities.

A judge who decides cases has no authority of capital punishment unless he is bearing witness. And in that case, he would not be the judge of that case. The responsibility of execution lies with the witnesses first, and then the rest of the population, judges and officials among them. This ensures that all the people are always recipients of the consequences they decide on in their courts—good or bad. If a judge decides on the death penalty in a case, and the public rightly disagrees, it's within their power and duty to refuse to continue the proceedings. If a judge makes a bad ruling, it is still the duty of the people to bear the consequences by blocking his decision and bearing the consequences—good or bad. There is no way out of this. If the people don't follow justice, they all bear the results together, spread across the whole community. The Pharisees understood this (though to evil ends) when they told Pilate that they would willingly suffer the consequences for crucifying Jesus (Matthew 27:25). If their response was ironically appropriate for putting an innocent man to death, wouldn't it also be appropriate for interposing to save an innocent man's life?

4. **The witnesses being required to cast the first stones emphasizes personal responsibility.**

This responsibility cannot be declined after witness testimony has been given to a judge. Refusing to cast the first stone would at least void the accusation if it were not considered tantamount to admission of bearing false witness. If a witness does not agree with this up front, then no accusation can be made at all. When a witness understands this immense responsibility, he will become invested in learning more about the whole process. He won't be content to leave the study of this wholly up to others, not if he has a conscience.

What is the bad fruit of not practicing lawful public stoning? The purpose of stoning is listed: "And all Israel shall hear and fear and never again do any such wickedness as this among you" (Deuteronomy 13:11). Deuteronomy 19:20 and 21:21 repeat a similar reason. So then if stoning is not practiced, a bad result will be produced. Either people won't fear to do evil as much as they should, or conversely, if a more severe form of execution is carried out (crucifixion, drawn and quartered, hanging executed bodies up for longer than a day [Deuteronomy 21:22-23], etc.), the people will become resentful for execution going too far and for authorities gloating over execution.

How can a city or any group of people be considered godly if it has no will (much less ability) to judge evildoers within itself? God's people are uncivilized, and we rely on a system that is largely ungodly to accomplish this. And it is often run by the ungodly also.

When a people is not afraid to commit capital offenses, trust (or rather refusing to trust) becomes a life-and-death issue. When people hear that evil is not dealt with quickly, they lock their cars, don't speak to strangers, won't give handouts to the poor, become uncomfortable with hospitality, and would never consider picking up a hitchhiker. The reasoning is that it's better to assume that a stranger will eventually damage himself and anyone who unduly trusts him. Society greatly fears being damaged by trusting people it shouldn't. The high cost of all these things is presumed to be unavoidable and is baked into the economy. This affects everything from the cost of a sandwich to getting a job to finding a spouse. How keen would you be to marry someone in a society where adultery is ignored by the courts?

When someone commits a capital offense that worldly governments view as evil enough, life in prison is usually upheld as the most loving option even though it produces a much less desirable result than God's design and at a much higher cost. If an offender spends forty years in prison and finally dies, that costs roughly forty years of wages to keep him alive and unable to do more harm, but in the end, the man is still dead, and the people will quickly forget about what he did. This is like a doctor diagnosing a patient and then giving the patient the option to pay extra *not* to hear the diagnosis, much less the treatment options. Who of sound mind would do this? Yet every one of the 3,000 plus counties in America is doing something like it every day, and the public pays the doctor's bill, as it were.

If that same man is publicly stoned to death, the public will not have to collectively pay forty years of wages in taxes, yes, but most importantly, the public will fear evildoing and will be much less likely to repeat it, and the man will be dead in the end either way. This swift and pointed justice will save more lives.

In both approaches, the public agrees that the offender is no longer trustworthy for the rest of his life. The current cost of keeping someone in prison for a year amounts to about the current average yearly income, depending on the jurisdiction. Taxes are levied on the public to pay these costs. To refuse to put someone quickly to death costs everyone a little. This is consistent with Leviticus 5:1; a person who fails to testify of evil will bear his guilt. A culture who refuses to obey God will face the judgment, the consequences. They work themselves out later in worse ways.

What is the bad fruit of stoning, and what is the good fruit of not stoning?

There are none. Any negative consequence that may come as a result of public stoning would actually be a result of practicing it improperly or maliciously. For example, let's say that someone is maliciously or mistakenly accused and put to death by stoning. This happened on account of Naboth's vineyard in 1 Kings 21:1-15. Is the law at fault because someone was wrongfully executed? Was the fault not with the people who made the malicious accusation?

But what if it was a serious mistake? The Bible is silent directly on the concept of mistaken accusations made in good faith that were not malicious, only that the principle of motive be taken into account for matters of what would otherwise be a capital offense (Numbers 35:22-25, Deuteronomy 19:19). People will make mistakes, but does that mean we shouldn't even attempt to uphold justice? Should we just quit trying since we can't be perfect?

For the other consequences which may appear negative such as ridicule, hardship, and persecution, these are also challenges that the righteous face. So if this position is indeed correct, these results are not outside the realm of expectation. When persecution is encountered for doing the right thing, persecution is a feature of obedience, not a punishment, for it turns away those without conviction (Deuteronomy 20:8, Judges 7:2) and is a sign of worthiness (Acts 5:40-42).

CHAPTER 6

We Died to the Law
We Establish

APPEALING TO THE LAW RAISES MANY key questions. It's important to understand the purpose of law so that the spirit of the law can be appropriately understood. Here are some of the most fundamental questions and answers.

Isn't this Judaizing?

Judaizers insist on circumcision of the flesh and obedience to gain justification in God's sight. This is backwards. The problem with the Galatians was that they rejected justification by faith and turned to justification by works (Galatians 5:4). Receiving living faith produces works; works do not produce faith. Just as a tree is made alive when the soil receives the seed, so a person is made alive when his heart is regenerated by faith. Relying on justification by works is as silly as stapling apples to a dead tree and saying, "It's alive!"

Trees bear fruit. The faith-full obey God by producing good works (James 2:14-26). Would you be upset at a living orange tree bearing oranges? How ignorant it would be to tell it that the fruit isn't what makes it alive! It's the seed from a previous piece of fruit that makes this particular tree alive. So God uses the faithful works of one man to sow the seeds of faith in another, and so on. There's nothing wrong with a murderer bearing the fruits of repentance, and there's nothing wrong with believers expecting this fruit from him. Just as a person plants a vineyard for grapes from the soil, so God planted Christ to produce good works from mankind (Ephesians 2:10, Philippians 2:12-13).

If repentance according to God's law is repulsive to you, you hate our Lord who died to meet the law's just requirement on our behalf. You are no child of His (Hosea 1:6-9).

Didn't we die to the law?

Correct, and by our faith, do we nullify the law? On the contrary, we establish and uphold the law which we are dead to (Romans 3:31, 7:4). People who break the law are under it. People who walk in the law are not under it. This is counter-intuitive, but this is the spirit of the law which penetrates the heart much more deeply than the letter. How do we know what sin is except in the light of the law? Why would we establish something we died to? For the believer, it's to produce the fruits of righteousness by faith. For the unbeliever, our fruits of obedience are simply the outward sign to them of our living faith by which we are made righteous (Deuteronomy 4:5-8).

Therefore, the fruit growing on a branch is not that tree's source of life, but it does display that it is alive. While the source of a tree's life is unseen, the fruits of its life ought to be clearly visible. So the law is good because it teaches us how to bear fruit.

The law does not kill; sin kills through the law (Romans 7:10-13). The law simply revealed the wages of sin, which is death. If an unbeliever does not know he is in sin while he is dead in his sin, he thinks he lives. This is a disservice to the unbeliever, for it allows him to continue in his sin and death, while being ignorant that he's dead. Try to convince a healthy person to undergo chemotherapy; you can't. Try to convince someone who is diagnosed with cancer; you can't stop him from giving everything if he has hope. Why would the living need a savior? Only the dead need Christ to give them life. The law is to humble us and show us that we're dead (Romans

7:9), and it's a tool, a schoolmaster to show us our need for faith in Christ. Christ is the doctor, and the law is his medical instrument. Sin is the cancer. To take that doctor's tools away, the guardian, the law away from unbelievers is a hateful thing to do. Don't remove the doctor's tools from his kit. That is wishing that they would not be healed and come to Christ (Galatians 3:24-29) through the knowledge of sin that the law imparts to them. The willing death of the flesh will give birth to the spirit of life. Knowledge of the law makes sin come alive to kill the unrighteous. For if the law is outside the heart, the heart produces sin leading to death. But if the law is in the heart, the heart produces righteousness leading to life. The power of Christ is that He's the only one who can place the law in the heart.

Wasn't the law the old covenant?

Correct, and the law is also the new covenant which we keep through Christ by the power of the Holy Spirit. There are 5 parts to a covenant:

1. Party A/The person who initiates the covenant (God)
2. Party B/The person who responds to the covenant (the nations through Israel)
3. The conditions (the law itself)

4. Blessings and curses for keeping it or breaking it, respectively (found in Deuteronomy 28)

5. Who will inherit the covenant? (children of those who keep it)

The new covenant has the same law as the old (Matthew 5:17-20). Jesus says this specifically, but there is also an image of this in the account of the tablets with the law. God gave Moses the law twice, signifying the old and new covenants. The first giving of the law was written on tablets of stone by God Himself. Moses took these down to the people, saw their idolatry and whoring after another god, and so he broke the tablets, the law, the covenant (Exodus 32:19). Then Moses went back up the mountain, and God tells him what to write. So God speaks to Moses, gives Moses His Word, and Moses writes the second copy himself. These tablets, with the exact same words as the first set (Exodus 34:1) were eventually to find their place inside the ark of the covenant, which was in the holy of holies, which was in the heart of the temple. Believers are that temple, and inside the ark resided the law, the bread from heaven, and the staff of Aaron the first high priest of Israel which God made to bud.

Therefore, just as Israel broke the old covenant, we have the same law of the new covenant placed within our hearts, for we are God's temple with Christ as the cornerstone. There is a law in the old covenant, and there is a law in the new, and they are the same. The old covenant is the law broken; the new covenant is the law obeyed. The new covenant consists of that same law being written on the tablets of our hearts (2 Corinthians 3:3, Jeremiah 31:31-33). Now we are free to walk in the spirit of the law, which does not conflict with the letter but which goes much deeper in its obedience. The only difference between the old and new covenant is a question of where the law resides. Does it reside outside the temple or inside? If outside the heart, the flesh will produce lawlessness (sin) and death. If inside the heart, the spirit will produce the fruits of righteousness and life which is why we were created in Christ (Ephesians 2:10).

Aren't we under grace, not the law (Romans 6:14)?

Amen, so let us live with the law written on our hearts since that is our identity in Christ. Only sinners are under the law, but those who have faith in Christ are not under the law but under grace. Anyone who sins wishes to put himself under the law, for the law is for the disobedient (1 Timothy 1:9). So whether or not someone is under law or grace depends on whether he is lawless in sin or obedient to the law by faith. If someone sins and says that he is under grace in sinning, he is under the law and is a liar. Therefore let us live obedient lives and produce evidence of grace and righteousness. The law teaches us how to be wise in carrying this out by faith, and the Holy Spirit enables us to do this.

The law is counter-intuitive to fallen man. Men who wish to be free of it bind themselves more tightly with its consequences. Those who wish to keep so close to it that it becomes written on their hearts will find liberty (James 1:22-25).

Isn't the law only for Israel?

The law is for the disobedient (1 Timothy 1:9). Is this speaking of only disobedient Israelites and not of all the disobedient? If only disobedient Israelites, how could God judge Sodom and Gomorrah with death, or any sinner with death for that matter? God judged Sodom and Gomorrah even before the law was given to Moses! We know that God judges the unrighteous (1 Corinthians 5:12). What does He judge them by? It must be by His standard (Romans 3:19). One of the ways the nations will see Israel as wise is through their obedience by faith (Deuteronomy 4:5-8).

But even if the law is only for Israel, who is Israel? Israel is Abraham's promised offspring. We know Christ is Abraham's offspring (Galatians 3:16), and so all who belong to Christ are Abraham's promised offspring (Galatians 3:29). Being a Jew is a matter of the heart (Romans 2:28-29). We have been grafted into Abraham's promises through Christ (Ephesians 2:11-22, 3:6, Romans 11:13-24). The physical descendants of Abraham will be grafted in again when the fullness of the nations has come (Romans 11:25).

The Greek word "ekklesia" which is often translated as "church" was used often along with "synagogue" in the Greek translation of the Scriptures made hundreds of years before Christ. These words simply refer to any group of people or things. This translation is called the Septuagint (usually abbreviated as LXX). The New Testament authors usually prefer to quote from this Greek translation rather than the original Hebrew text of the Scriptures. Even when Stephen was on trial, he refers to the "ekklesia" ("church") in the wilderness with Moses (Acts 7:38). Some translations render this as "assembly," "congregation," or "gathering" which is all "church" means. Stephen is not referring to the nations but to the "gathering" of Israel in this specific instance based on the context.

Several passages from the Septuagint use the word "ekklesia" when referring to God's people (Judges 20:2, Lamentations 1:10, and Joel 2:16). Some say "ekklesia of Israel" specifically (Deuteronomy 31:30 and Joshua 8:35). Scripture speaks of the "ekklesia of evildoers" (Psalm 26:5). A passage uses "ekklesia" and "synagogue" as synonyms (Proverbs 5:14). So it makes no sense to place a dichotomy between the church ("ekklesia") and Israel. If someone wanted to be pedantic, when someone says church, you could ask, "church of what?" Colloquially, when we say "church" (meaning "group") we mean a group of God's people. God's church or "ekklesia" is Israel and always has been at least since Abraham if not before. Those not of Abraham's bloodline have always been able to be grafted into Israel. It just so happens today that that's the most common path to becoming a child of Abraham, but it's nothing special (Romans 11:21). In terms of learning about God, compared to being a physical Israelite who believes, it's a disadvantage to be grafted into Israel from the nations (Romans 9:3-5). But it's still infinitely better than being an unbelieving Israelite.

The LXX (Septuagint) was commonly used in Jesus's time. Were these translators working before Christ guilty of holding "replacement theology?" Was Stephen? God has only ever had one true people: those who keep His commandments (Hosea 1:9). So even if the law was only for Israel, that means that the law is for believers in Christ.

In 1 Corinthians 9:8-14, Paul makes it clear that he has a right to be paid for his ministry, that he says these things on the authority of the Law of Moses, and that it was written for the sake of believers. So we know the law is for the believer and the disobedient alike.

Doesn't Ephesians 2:15 say that the law of commandments in ordinances has been abolished?

The Greek work translated as "ordinances" is "dogma-sin." It does not say the law has been abolished, or even that the law of commandments has been abolished. It only says that the law of commandments *in ordinances* has been abolished. We know what laws are, and we know what commandments are. What are ordinances or "dogmasin?"

The word is only used five times in the New Testament. The word is never used to refer to God's law or commandments anywhere in Scripture.

In the New Testament:

- A decree of Caesar (Luke 2:1)
- Decisions reached by elders and apostles (Acts 16:4)
- A decree of Caesar (Acts 17:7)
- What is abolished in Christ's flesh (Ephesians 2:15)
- A written account of violations that has been nailed to the cross (Colossians 2:14)

In the Greek translation of the Old Testament that the Jews made for themselves (referred to as the LXX or Septuagint), the word "dogma" is only used in the book of Daniel. The Hebrew word is "esar" which is also only used in Daniel:

- Dogma by Nebuchadnezzar to kill the wise men who could not interpret his dream (2:13)
- Dogma by Nebuchadnezzar that the people should commit idolatry before a golden calf when they hear the designated music (3:10)
- Dogma by Nebuchadnezzar that anyone who speaks against the God of the Jews should be torn limb from limb and his house laid in ruins (3:29)
- Dogma by Nebuchadnezzar that the wise men of Babylon should be brought to interpret his dream (4:6)
- Dogma that King Darius signed establishing that anyone who prays to anyone other than himself for the next thirty days should be thrown into a den of lions (6:8-15)
- Dogma by King Darius that his people are to fear Daniel's God (6:26)

So we see the word is never used to refer to God's law. The law of commandments expressed in ordinances is a written decree. Ordinances (dogmasin) can be according to God's law or not. Regardless, it is nailed to the cross. This includes the records of debt against us that are lawful according to God's law, and those that are unlawful according to God's law. The law of commandments contained in decrees has been abolished in every regard (according to God and the decisions and decrees of men) because of the cross.

Should I obey law XYZ?

One common view is that we can assume that no law from Moses continues unless expressly repeated in the New Testament. Examples of these laws would include Leviticus 19:14 about cursing the deaf or putting a stumbling block before the blind, Exodus 23:4-5 about returning a lost animal to its owner or helping an enemy's fallen ox under its load, Exodus 22:6 that requires an arsonist to pay for the damages of the fire he kindled, and Leviticus 20:15-16 which lists the death penalty for lying sexually with an animal. This argument is absurd and directly contradicts Jesus's words in Matthew 5:17-20 that says we are not even allowed to think that he came to relax the law in the smallest degree.

Given this understanding, there are a million questions here which are all great questions that have answers that are not within the scope of any book other than Scripture itself. To attempt to answer them all is every man's personal responsibility to seek out (Micah 6:8). Simply, the answer for every law is: yes. Each question deserves more than a large book and even more public discussion, but that is not the focus here. There are many things to discuss about the nature of circumcision, tassels, cutting off a woman's hand, and many more. Here are abridged answers to the three most common ones.

Should I abstain from pork and shellfish and keep the feasts and festivals?

We are not permitted to defile ourselves by what we eat. Before Christ, coming into contact with unclean things, certainly eating unclean things, would defile a person (Leviticus 11, Haggai 2:10-14). When Christ came, due to His indestructible life (Hebrews 7:16), anything He touched did not defile him, but was itself made clean. Anyone besides the high priest who entered the holy of holies on the day of atonement was killed by God because they were not fit to serve Him; they were unclean. Christ is that High Priest, and in Ezekiel 47:1-12, water issues forth from underneath the threshold of the temple through Christ's sacrifice. Everywhere this water flows, it turns salt water to fresh and produces life, fish, and trees with fruit and leaves for healing. Before Christ, we were not fit to serve God, and if His presence came out to us, it would kill us, but through Christ's offering on the cross, the life and healing from the law, the manna, and Aaron's rod in the holy of holies comes out to the world. It heals us and does not kill us now. As Christ said, nothing outside a person can defile him by going in to him (Mark 7:15). This immediately brings up all the unclean foods mentioned in Leviticus 11. In verses 41-45, we are told that eating unclean things will make us defiled. Is Christ contradicting the law? May it never be.

Moreover, Christ also teaches us that doing good works is truly eating (John 4:34). So ultimately, eating what is clean is to bear the fruits of faith, which is good works. Food is a shadow of works. Jesus said that the evil works which a man does is what defiles himself. Sinning by thought, word, or deed is eating what is unclean. The bread and wine are Christ's body and blood. Eating and drinking these things reminds us to follow Christ in His works, His sufferings. Then He comes to dwell in us, as food does in the stomach, but Christ in the heart. You are what you eat. You are what you therefore do. God is known by His works, and we are to be also.

The Holy Spirit also instructs us through Paul: "Therefore let no one pass judgment on you in questions of food and drink, or with regard to a festival or a new moon or a Sabbath, which are a shadow of the things to come, but the body is Christ" (Colossians 2:16-17). In the question of clean and unclean food, this is a shadow, and Christ is the body. Related to this, drinking blood meant that a man was to be cut off from his people (Leviticus 7:27, 17:14) which required being put to death in some cases if not all (Exodus 31:14). By drinking

Christ's blood spiritually, we are cut off from our people and are made alive to God. By eating His flesh spiritually, we become one body with Him. We are cut off from the wild olive tree and grafted into Abraham (Romans 11:17). So to eat something unclean, that would mean that I am not eating Christ's flesh, meaning I am not doing his works, not of His body and do not belong to Him. God's Word is true food, and His blood is true drink (John 6:51-60). To receive words not from God is eating what is unclean.

1 Timothy 4:1-5 also clarifies that nothing created by God should be rejected if it is received with thanksgiving, but it is made holy by the word of God and prayer. Before Christ, a man would be made unholy and bear unclean offspring if he were joined in marriage to a non-Israelite or non-sojourning woman. But in the new covenant, it is clear that the believing spouse makes the unbelieving (non-Israelite) spouse holy, and therefore the children are holy (1 Corinthians 7:14). If cleansing by touch applies to a man lying with his wife, would this not also be true of what we eat? Let everyone be fully convinced in his own mind.

Should we offer animal sacrifices?

The scope of offerings has been greatly expanded. However, no believer alive today is under the priestly order of Aaron. At best, offering animal sacrifices would be a pointless activity. At worst, it would be offering strange fire (Leviticus 10). We operate under the priesthood of Melchizedek (Hebrews 7:15-17). We offer our own bodies as Christ did (Romans 12:1). We also offer sacrifices of praise (Hebrews 13:15).

Furthermore, believers are now God's dwelling place in a way not previously known. The Spirit dwells in us ever since Christ sent the Holy Spirit on the day of Pentecost. In that sense, everywhere a believer goes is the entrance to the tent of meeting, for we are that tent of meeting. Our earthly bodies are now the representatives of the heavenly temple as Christ's own body was. We are His body.

So believers offer themselves as sacrifice on the altar. This concept is known as the priesthood of the believer. Believers are priests (1 Peter 2:9, Revelation 1:6, 5:10, 20:6). And we will make offerings forever. If we were not such priests, day and night would have ceased with the destruction of the second temple in 70 A.D. (Jeremiah 33:14-22). We are also living stones of the temple (1 Peter 2:4-5). So every believer is a fully functioning temple sacrificial system walking on two legs, fully equipped to bear the fruits of Christ's atonement by offering ourselves in an acceptable manner to forgive one another and the nations. Animal sacrifices and the temple made with hands are the wrong priesthood. We now serve according to the body of the temple, the one made without hands, that is, our bodies.

Can I kill you for breaking Sabbath?

If I am breaking the sabbath, it means I am not a priest and have not entered Christ's sabbath rest and would most likely be outside the jurisdiction of God's nation unless I were a sojourner. If I were in the jurisdiction of God's nation due to being a priest (that is, a believer), priests profane the Sabbath and are guiltless (Matthew 12:1-8). We have entered, must strive to enter, and will enter Christ's rest by faith (Hebrews 4:1-11). We are priests serving in the true temple. Therefore, we profane the Sabbath by offering our bodies as living sacrifices and are therefore guiltless also. If a priest in the temple is guiltless in his priestly work on the sabbath, how much more is a priest who is part of the temple who offers himself as a living sacrifice!

Christ's work is our rest, so our work is the world's rest. For a believer to break the Sabbath, that would be rejecting Christ after receiving His name. Hebrews 6:4-8 tells us that if someone has been enlightened and then falls away, it is impossible to restore him again to repentance. God will judge those outside the camp.

Failing to be circumcised was a capital offense (Genesis 17:14 says to cut off, Exodus 31:14 says putting to death for breaking the sabbath is cutting off, and Numbers 15:32-36 is them performing it). Paul tells us that flesh circumcision and uncircumcision are both nothing, only keeping God's commandments (1 Corinthians 7:19). Circumcision is one change in the law that Hebrews speaks of. If one cutting off offense has "been spiritualized," to mean circumcision in the heart is sufficient (Deuteronomy 10:16), why would another "cut off" offense not be, especially seeing as priests who profane it in their service are guiltless? Eating blood was another "cut off" offense, and yet it is a requirement to abide in Christ (Leviticus 17:10, John 6:56).

What about the threefold distinction?

Some will bring up a popular way of understanding the law known as the threefold distinction. This argument says that there are three categories of law: moral, ceremonial, and judicial (or civil). The basic form of this argument says that the ceremonial and judicial aspects of the law are no longer in effect, that only the moral laws are still binding. Thomas Aquinas and the Westminster Confession of Faith are most notably attributed for presenting this view. I do not see such a distinction.

Now we do know there is a change in the law that took place with the change in priesthood from Aaron to Melchizedek (Hebrews 7:12). It is clear that Scripture does make a distinction between shadow and body. In Colossians 2:16-17 Paul lists four things which are shadows: matters of food and drink, new moons, festivals, and Sabbaths. All the laws still apply to everyone everywhere. We now have the substance of these things which are specifically listed: temple service, matters of food and drink, new moons, festivals, Sabbaths. Christ is the body of these things, and we are members of Christ's body.

Otherwise, what would the standard be? Let's say only the moral law applies but the judicial laws do not. What do we do when a murder is witnessed? Ask him not to do it again and let him go? Do we go to law before unbelievers against him which Paul specifically prohibits in 1 Corinthians 5-6? Do we get to make up our own version of slavery and lock him in prison at the innocent public's expense? By what standard? If God's word does not tell us how to act in these areas, what do we do?

Scripture does use the law of capital punishment as the basis for putting our sin to death in sanctification (Colossians 3:5, Romans 8:13). I believe it also translates to excommunication as a form of "cutting off" which Scripture uses as a synonym with capital punishment (Leviticus 20:2-3).

So if there is one case against the body carrying out capital punishment, it should at least look like permanent excommunication, and especially if the person is unrepentant. But this ignores the question for: what if the person repents? Jesus commended Zacchaeus for willingly paying what the law requires for his offenses. This was his evidence of repentance. Let's say that a murderer is repentant: should his payment be excommunication? Aren't only the unrepentant supposed to be excommunicated? What if we excommunicated a person, thereby "killing" him, and then immediately allowed re-fellowshipping him so that he's "resurrected" to life? How many times can he do this? Isn't this a cop-out?

I think the final option is missing: voluntarily agreeing to be put to death rather than face excommunication. Wouldn't this be an extraordinary testimony to the world? It would cause them to ask what would persuade someone to accept death for his wrongdoing when he has the option to simply be excommunicated. Losing community needs to have some serious teeth. The church body is largely numb and disconnected. Most of us don't even know what it would be like to have true national identity in Christ. I imagine even very few Americans would rather die instead of effectively having their citizenship revoked. Our loyalty to one another as God's people needs to be much stronger.

CHAPTER 7

Scriptural Challenges

What about the Sermon on the Mount? Didn't Jesus say to turn the other cheek? Shouldn't we just forgive those worthy of death?

Jesus tells us not to resist an evil person in the Sermon on the Mount. "You have heard that it was said, 'An eye for an eye and a tooth for a tooth.' But I say to you, Do not resist the one who is evil. But if anyone slaps you on the right cheek, turn to him the other also. And if anyone would sue you and take your tunic, let him have your cloak as well. And if anyone forces you to go one mile, go with him two miles. Give to the one who begs from you, and do not refuse the one who would borrow from you" (Matthew 5:38-40).

Jesus is not contradicting the law here. He is offering the satisfaction for its requirement. Godly forgiveness is always based on payment, on atonement. If it were not, God could pardon without Christ's death. God can't cheat Himself; He is perfectly just, and payment must be made. When someone strikes a person, the law says that stripe for stripe is the appropriate payment. Jesus is teaching that payment can be made at the expense of the victim. This is exactly what God did through Christ. We robbed God by stealing ourselves from His authority. So how does He regain this authority? He suffers again just like in the parable of the lost sheep (Matthew 18:12-14, Luke 15:3-7). The sheep runs away, robbing its master of his property. The shepherd doesn't cut his losses; he uses his own resources to regain what was lost. The sheep didn't return itself in this instance.

So when Jesus says to turn the other cheek or go the extra mile, it is commanding us to offer payment for wrongs committed against us to satisfy justice. This is all that mercy is: satisfying justice on someone else's behalf. For example: Let's say a man named Viktor steals Penny's coat, and Penny gives him another one. A week passes. So when Viktor is caught and brought to justice, the penalty is for Viktor to return two coats to Penny. Viktor already has the one he stole from

Penny, so he returns that. Where does he get the other coat that he must add to it to satisfy justice? He got the second one from Penny which she gave him at the time of the robbery. In the end, Penny will have both coats back that were originally hers, and Viktor will not owe her any coats. He's restored to his original status before his theft.

Also, we must note that Jesus doesn't use examples of capital offenses. He doesn't say, "If anyone should murder your wife, let him murder your daughter." He leaves it to cases of property theft, non-lethal violence, and forced labor. There is no prohibition for us to make payment on behalf of others for things at this level. But we are prohibited from putting a substitute to death for the life of a murderer (Numbers 35:30-33). This is God's right alone to substitute Himself for matters of life and death, since He is the only one who has His own life to give. God owns Himself; men do not. Scripture refers to self-stewardship under God, not outright self-ownership as if we had alodial titles to our lives, as it were (John 8:34, Romans 6:20-22, 1 Peter 2:16). Does this also apply to all kinds of capital offenses? I don't know, but at least in the case of murder and devoting to destruction (the ban), Scripture is clear.

When someone steals, we can exemplify the gospel by paying a thief's debt. This is redemption and atonement. This holds true for all sins that do not lead to death.

However, when dealing with matters of capital punishment, putting the guilty person to death is redemption and atonement. God reserves the ability to redeem someone from the dead for Himself alone. Murderers cannot be redeemed by ransom or substitute (Numbers 35:31). And those under the ban who have been devoted to destruction are also unable to be redeemed by ransom, but they are to be put to death for atonement (Leviticus 1:4, 27:28-29, Deuteronomy 13:16).

If this were not the case, someone who claims Christ could be cut off (excommunicated), someone else could suffer that fate as a substitute on the offender's behalf, and then the person could repeat the process indefinitely until none were left in the congregation. He could invoke "forgive not seven times, but seventy seven times" (Matthew 18:21-22). A single person could theoretically utilize the mercy of hundreds of people to kill them all according to the law. This is nonsense.

God, on the other hand, cannot be dismantled. He bought those who continue to deny Him (2 Peter 2:1), and by His power combined with their continuing unbelief, His death fuels their eternal death by the power of His eternal life.

So since atonement for sin has already been achieved through Christ, we must evidence that by paying for (redeeming) everything that is within our power to pay. This does not include murder or offenses that result in the ban. God's law gives certain limits on our ability to pay on behalf of wrongdoers in this life. Christ's sacrifice has no such limits. While men may be alive spiritually through Christ's death, we still die physically and must pay debts for wrongs. This will be true until the fullness of the Kingdom is come when there will be no more sin. Otherwise, a man could steal with reckless abandon and argue that he doesn't have to pay for it since Christ paid for it.

Shouldn't a repentant believer want to pay his debts and then produce wealth and forgiveness for others through righteous deeds? What does repentance look like for capital offenses? For God's people, it looks like putting offenders to death in great fear so that it may not happen again.

What about the Sermon on the Mount, where Jesus said looking at a woman with lust is adultery in the heart? Should people be stoned for that or murder in the heart (Matthew 5:21-28)?
To be sure, all sin is worthy of death, even sin in the heart. It's also important to note that punishing someone with court proceedings does not satisfy God's eternal justice. Temporal or earthly justice is merely a shadow and a copy of eternal, heavenly justice. If someone were to live a perfectly sinless life, but then he steals something and

is brought to justice in an earthly court, he is still worthy of eternal death in God's eyes. Earthly justice does not save anyone. It is simply showing the fruit of our righteousness by faith as works. And it's an example for the unbelievers to see God's justice displayed since they only have earthly eyes to see.

However, not all sin is to be punished the same way bodily. All sin leads to death, but God has not placed a responsibility on us to put people to death (or even punish at all) for most sins, and certainly not sins of the heart that do not bear fruit as actions. People cannot witness the intentions of a man's heart except by that man's action. Only God can judge the heart, and He indeed will on the day of judgment. Man can only bear witness of outward appearances. God sees the heart (1 Samuel 16:7).

What about the woman caught in adultery (John 7:53-8:11)? It is important to note that this passage currently has one of the most dubious reputations in the New Testament as far as its Scriptural authenticity is concerned. It does not appear in any surviving manuscripts at all until 384 A.D. in Latin. It has not been found in a Greek manuscript earlier than 400-600 A.D, and not in a reliable Greek manuscript until the 700s A.D. For this reason, I am not convinced that John 7:53-8:11 is Scripture. We must use the certain passages to understand the uncertain, and it is unwise to change the entire understanding of Scripture by a single passage, and a highly doubtful one at that. There is no other passage that is held as such an authority on the topic of repealing the validity of all death penalties. This is an inconsistent approach to Scripture.

Even so, for the sake of due diligence, let's assume John 7:53-8:11 is indeed authentic. The Pharisees attempt to put Jesus between the two horns of a dilemma as they love to do. Their goal was to pressure him either to violate the laws of Moses which would upset the Jews or to violate Roman law by inciting an execution that Rome did not authorize. Roman law prohibited Jewish executions without permission (with rare exception). I think it most likely they thought Jesus would take the second option. The Pharisees wanted to call attention that obedience to God's law would cause much hardship for anyone who wished to obey it. This was especially true during that time of God's judgment with Roman occupation, and it's still true today.

There are several issues with this:

1. It takes a woman and a man to commit adultery, at least one of whom must be married. If she was caught in the act, where was the man she was found with? He should have been brought

forward also. The Pharisees seemed to uphold
Moses, but they proved that they did not believe
Moses. The Pharisees' problem wasn't that they
held to the laws of Moses, but rather that they
didn't believe Moses. This is why they rejected
Jesus (John 4:46-47).

2. Jesus was not a judge in Israel. He is indeed the
    judge of the world and will come again to judge
    it, but He did not come to judge the world (i.e. the
    disobedient) at His first coming (John 3:17, 12:47).
    The Pharisees were pulling a stunt by asking some-
    one who was not a judge in Israel to offer an opin-
    ion. Even if Jesus had said to stone her, she would
    still need to be taken to a judge, and if declared
    guilty, the eyewitnesses would have to throw the
    first stone at her, and only then Jesus would have
    needed to follow suit. He was not an eyewitness.

3. If Jesus was repealing the death penalty, then
    this conundrum doesn't make much sense for
    the Pharisees to present to Jesus because Jesus
    accused the Pharisees of rejecting Moses's laws
    commanding the stoning of rebellious children
    (Mark 7:9-13). What sense would it make for the
    Pharisees to pose this dichotomy to Him when
    Jesus already condemned them for not executing
    rebellious children because of their traditions?

Jesus said that they made the word of God void by their traditions.

Setting these issues aside, the arguments against stoning based off this passage argue that only those without sin can stone someone for adultery. The argument then continues that if it applies for adultery, it also applies to every other offense that involved stoning. But then the argument abruptly stops. Proponents of this understanding do not advocate for the abolition of prison (as this book does, though for different reasons). And many who argue that this passage abolishes stoning still see the death penalty as mandatory or agree with a life-long prison sentence. Why is this? If Jesus said that no one who has ever sinned can stone another, did He contradict Himself when he said to first remove the log from your own eye so that you may see clearly to remove the speck from your brother's eye? Wouldn't that teaching become "get the log out of your own eye, and you now have no right to remove the speck from your brother's eye"?

Wouldn't this reasoning continue that now no one can ever be punished for anything at the hands of anyone? Or why would this apply to serious offenses only and not to small ones, or why just stoning? Wouldn't this reasoning state that punishments must be abolished for adultery and blasphemy as well as everything else down to trivial matters? This last question is the most consistent, especially when Matthew 5:38-42 is considered regarding turning the other cheek.

The proper question must become this: What does forgiveness for a capital offense consist of? The answer is payment. Someone must die. Jesus did die in the place of adulteresses. This places the law in the heart, so that now a person like Zacchaeus will want to pay what the law requires. And Paul would agree that he should be put to death with due process if he deserved it (Acts 25:11). The saved person wants to right his own wrongs so he can then right the wrongs that others commit. As an aside, it can be argued that Paul was a murderer for putting Christians to death, but that was not something the Jews would have accused him of; they agreed with him in this persecution of Christians since it was the priests who commissioned him to do it (Acts 26:9-11).

This account is not a requirement to let everyone else off the hook because we're sinful. It is to make us fear God and walk uprightly, for if we do not, we cannot offer justice to those who need it. We will be forgiven to the same measure we forgive others. The goal is not to be forgiving so we may sin more. But it is a realization that we have already been forgiven much, so we are obligated to forgive with God's forgiveness. Our debts were canceled by Christ, so we have a new creditor. As the hymn goes, "Jesus paid it all. All to Him I owe." We may not use our forgiveness as a cover-up for evil, but we must walk in freedom towards men as slaves to God (1 Peter 2:16). Christ has removed our sin from us as believers. So if anyone should be able to judge uprightly, it is believers. Let him who is without sin cast the first stone. This is a call for us to be blameless as believers. We are to judge angels in the next life. How much more are we meant to judge matters in this life (1 Corinthians 6:2-3)! In comparison to judging angels, capital trials in this life are trivial.

Jesus was sinless and still did not stone her though. Why is this? Firstly, he upheld the witness requirements from Deuteronomy 13:9 and 17:7. The two or three witnesses must cast first. Jesus said he did not condemn her because she had no witnesses to condemn her (John 8:10-11). Eyewitnesses must bring the charges. Jesus could not condemn her since he was not an eyewitness and was only a single person, not two or three. While He is fully God, He is also fully man and kept the law perfectly. This passage still has too much weight given to it on this topic.

Jesus did uphold the law of capital punishment at that time, but the new covenant had not yet come until after his death. Wasn't He teaching still under the ministry of the law, the old covenant?

If the answer to this is yes, then the previous objection related to the woman caught in adultery in John 7:53-8:11 can no longer be used.

Yet Jesus said in Matthew 12:28 and Luke 11:20 that if He cast out demons by the Spirit of God and the finger of God, that the kingdom of God is upon us. So to use this argument, according to Jesus, you must also reject that Jesus cast out demons by the Spirit of God. And even still, were significant parts of His teaching about to be undone or abolished after His resurrection or at Pentecost? Would he have to clarify or retract thousands of points He made in the forty days between His resurrection and ascension? Was His teaching not already a radical fulfillment of the law with all authority? The new covenant consists of the law being written on our hearts (Jeremiah 31:33). Scripture says that we establish and uphold the law by our faith (Romans 3:31).

We believe that a person should be able to take responsibility for all the good things he does. He gets to choose what to do with the fruits of his labor and how to raise his children, or at least everyone desires to. Yet it's human nature since the fall to refuse responsibility for the evil fruit a person produces. The options are both or neither.

Job had a new-covenant-attitude in Job 1:5 where he offered sacrifices on behalf of his children just in case they had done something to make it necessary. Job lived before the Levitical priesthood, and so was under a Melchizedekian priesthood or maybe even a priesthood before Melchizedek. While Job himself was innocent of his children's sins, God considered him the most upright person on earth, and this was part of the reason why. So even absent the old covenant, to be considered righteous before God, a person must exemplify a spirit of bearing the consequences for what others do. This has not changed between the covenants. An upright person in God's eyes is someone who takes responsibility for others. This is God's test that His own son passed.

If someone's deeds produce death or curses, and yet is not meant to take responsibility, then for consistency, if someone's deeds produce life or blessings, he is also not meant to take responsibility. This is what God gives us. If we refuse to take responsibility for our evil, God will bring in oppression on us so that we may not have responsibility over our good works either.

What about the prison in Jesus's parable of the unforgiving servant (Matthew 18:23-35)?

In this parable, the king has a servant who owes him 10,000 talents, roughly 200,000 years of wages for a day laborer. The king orders his servant to be sold along with his wife, children, and all his possessions to pay the debt. The servant pleads with the king, and the king has mercy on the servant and eats the expense, thereby forgiving the servant. The servant then goes and attempts to collect payment of one hundred denarii, roughly one hundred days' wages from another servant. The second servant pleads for mercy, but the first servant has him put under prison guard until he can repay. The king calls the first servant back and condemns him with the same judgment that he put upon the second servant, placing the original 10,000 talent debt upon him and handing him over to the prison torturers.

Does Jesus uphold the lawfulness of prison with this parable? The king represents God (verses 34-35). The king was not going to punish the first servant with prison originally. He ordered the servant to be sold into slavery, not imprisoned (verse 25). Anyone who buys a man will undoubtedly put him into service. He won't waste the price he paid to then have the man not be of valuable service to him. The king only handed his servant over to the prison torturers (verse 34) because that was the punishment that the servant sought to do to another. The punishment matched the heart intent of the first servant (Deuteronomy 19:16-21, Matthew 7:2).

What about Paul telling the Corinthians to restore the sinner in 2 Corinthians 2:5-11?

There is a great deal of uncertainty as to who Paul referred to, what he had done, and to whom. He mentions something he wrote in a previous letter. Was it the same man he referred to of a capital offense in 1 Corinthians 5?

Was it in another letter that we don't know about? Was it Alexander the coppersmith? Was it someone else un-named who confronted Paul about his authority during one of his visits to Corinth?

It seems highly unlikely that it was the capital offender who took his father's wife in 1 Corinthians 5. Paul speci-fies that the person (he doesn't say man) who caused pain has not caused pain to Paul himself, but to that congre-gation. Why would Paul feel the need to specify that the man taking his father's wife was not causing pain to him? Of course he wasn't causing him pain. That wasn't an offense committed against Paul. This doesn't follow. He also says he doesn't want to state this too severely. But if this is the same situation, why did Paul not hesitate previ-ously to call for the congregation to hand the man over to Satan for the destruction of the flesh so that his soul may be saved? This is the most severe pronouncement.

Yet unless names or details are known for certain, it's not possible to comment on this with any confidence one way or another. If it can be shown that Paul is in-deed referring to a capital offender, it would certainly void many thoughts in this book.

What about the letter to the gentile believers in Acts 15:1–31?
The apostles wrote a letter to new non-Jewish believers in nearby cities shortly after Christ's ascension. The

new covenant caused a new growing pain for the faith. Jews had been raised to learn the law from a young age and had great opportunity to learn it and be guarded by their parents from serious sin. But now thousands of adults were coming to faith more quickly than ever and at great distance from those who had a functional knowledge of the law. The disciples held a council to discuss what to teach people during this rapid growth.

Here was another opportunity for Paul and the other apostles and elders to tell the new converts not to worry about the law if they could safely ignore it due to being "under grace." Yet they didn't. What were the things they encouraged them to do?

1. Abstain from food sacrificed to idols.
2. Abstain from blood.
3. Abstain from what has been strangled.
4. Abstain from sexual immorality.

What was this list for? We know that later in the epistles, Paul tells us that idols are nothing, and so food sacrificed to idols is acceptable to eat for those who are mature in faith (1 Corinthians 8:4). Scripture directly prohibits eating blood under threat of being cut off, though many believers today hardly know about this, much less give it any thought. The strangulation prohibition appears to be a tradition. There is no law in

Scripture about abstaining from eating strangled things, only to be sure to pour out the blood from meat and cover it with dirt (Leviticus 17:13). Strangling an animal before draining the blood makes it harder to remove the blood instead of cutting the animal open and letting the animal's heart pump out the blood. So it seems to be a tradition added as a precaution. And for the last item, everyone agrees that sexual immorality is as wrong as it ever was. So why are there three categories of requirements here?

They should be categorized respectively:

1. Do not make others stumble by your liberty.
2. Do not sin (penalty is being cut off).
3. Do not break a tradition that's a good idea.
4. Do not sin (penalties range between legal fines and death).

One understanding that could make sense is that it was a simple and effective way to promote harmony between Jewish believers and believers from the nations. But the main question that needs to be answered here is this: is this a definitive or complete list for how non-ethnic Jews are to live? If so, then stealing, assault, bearing false witness, and anything else not mentioned need to be considered fully righteous acts now. Yet Paul excommunicated men for blasphemy (1 Timothy 1:20). This leads to an absurd and contradictory conclusion, so the answer must be no.

CHAPTER 8

Jurisdiction in a Nation "Without Borders"

IF YOU HAVE SPENT MUCH TIME talking about strife and disagreements within the body of believers, you have likely heard of "irreconcilable" differences over anything between the color of carpet in a meeting space to capital offenses and what to do about these differences. In cases where there are people being removed from the body, the excommunicated party will usually go down the street in the same town to another group who knows nothing of the situation that led to the cutting off. Christ's body is one, yet we are practically dismembered, nearly unaware of what goes on next door. The pinky doesn't sense the ring finger's painful infection. The infection that got so advanced that an amputation was necessary, and the dismembered and cancerous finger goes looking for somewhere else to re-attach itself; all too often it succeeds.

For these reasons, it's important to be familiar with the concept of jurisdiction as Scripture uses it. Deuteronomy 21:1-9 details a situation where a slain person is found. The procedure in verses 2-3 is the law's definition of juris-diction. Whatever city is nearest to where the body was found, that is the city whose judges, elders, and priests are responsible to act. This means that every area on earth is covered by some city's priests, elders, and officials.

We also see this idea in Deuteronomy 20 in the laws for warfare being laid out at the city level. The highest level of earthly jurisdiction is designed by God to end ideally at the city level. Higher jurisdictions are God's judgment of some failure on the part of a city: county, state, federal, international. Even Israel's kingdom was the result of moral failure on the part of God's people (1 Samuel 8). War is to be made on a city-by-city basis. It is not necessarily the case that a neighboring city should also receive the same treatment merely because it be-longs to the same nation.

In Judges 19-20, we see the story of the sexual viola-tion and murder of a Levite's concubine by men of the city of Gibeah in the tribe of Benjamin. The Levite cut his concubine's body into twelve pieces and sent them throughout the twelve tribes. The tribes had never seen anything like this and assembled 400,000 fighting men to decide what to do. They sent men throughout the whole tribe of Benjamin urging them to give up the worthless murderers for judgment. When the tribe of Benjamin refused, the rest of Israel made war against the city of Gibeah (not the while tribe of Benjamin), and God confirmed that war was appropriate when they inquired of Him (Judges 20:12-23). This also makes allowance for what some would call a civil war, that is, war within a nation to deal with an iniquitous city.

We (believers) have had city authority stripped from us for disobedience. (Stripped might be speaking of ourselves too generously. We have largely given it away.) We are citizens of the heavenly city, and that can never be taken away, but on this earth, city authority can be and has been. So now what? Believers are sprinkled like salt throughout the whole world. Where should the church's jurisdiction begin and end, and up to what weight or severity of offense? How can we possibly keep track of so many jurisdictions? The answer is beautifully simple.

1. Those who bear Christ's name are within our jurisdiction (1 Corinthians 5:11).

2. Those who do not bear Christ's name are outside our jurisdiction (1 Corinthians 5:12-13).

In 1 Corinthians 5:11-13 Paul asks a pair of questions and gives a pair of respective answers. If we pair each answer with each question respectively, it looks like this:

1. "For what have I to do with judging outsiders?" The implied answer is "nothing" because "God judges those outside."

2. "Is it not those inside whom you are to judge?" The implied answer is "definitely," therefore "Purge the evil person from among you."[1]

At the risk of sounding redundant, we can use these two points to answer every situation:

Q: What if a believer commits an offense against another believer?

A: "Is it not those inside whom you are to judge?"

Q: What if an unbeliever commits an offense against another unbeliever?

A: "For what have I to do with judging outsiders?"

Q: What if a believer commits a capital offense?

A: "Is it not those inside whom you are to judge?"

Q: What if an unbeliever commits a capital offense?

A: "For what have I to do with judging outsiders?"

1. Paul quotes verbatim from the Greek Septuagint, Deuteronomy 13:5; 17:7, 12; 19:19; 21:21; 22:21-24; and 24:7, every instance of which is only referring to public execution.

Q: What if a believer commits an offense against an
      unbeliever?

A: "Is it not those inside whom you are to judge?"

Q: What if an unbeliever commits an offense
      against a believer?

A: "For what have I to do with judging outsiders?"

So we see a clear concept of jurisdiction here with Paul speaking of those inside and those outside, and bearing Christ's name makes the difference. Of course there are those who falsely bear Christ's name or those who don't claim Christ but want to reap the benefits as if they were in the body, and those would be akin to sojourners in Israel, that is, we judge them the same (Exodus 12:49, Numbers 15:16). God knows the heart, but we must judge based upon a person's confession of who Christ is.

This concept may also provide a simple answer to what would otherwise be a difficult question:

If God's people are supposed to be executing capital offenders according to Moses, why didn't Paul also call for the purging of those who were previously idolaters, adulterers, and practicing homosexuals in the same group of believers just a few verses later (1 Corinthians 6:9)?

The answer goes right back to jurisdiction. If someone commits a murder in one jurisdiction and flees or travels to another, he is judged by the officials in the jurisdiction where the offense was committed (Deuteronomy 21:3), not the jurisdiction of whatever city he escapes to. Even for the manslayer with the avenger (redeemer) of blood, it made no difference where he fled in regard to who his redeemer was or who the congregation judging him was (Numbers 35:24-25). Without this principle, any wrong-doer could pick his judges after the fact, basing his choice on who would be most likely to rule in his favor. He could just flee there.

Those who were guilty of capital offenses before bearing Christ's name will be judged based on the juris-diction in which the offense was committed. So for an unbeliever who then becomes a believer, God will judge him for outside offenses. Other believers are not called to take on this responsibility. Now that he is a believer who bears Christ's name, he should be judged by us for things done among us (Hebrews 10:26). Furthermore, John is consistent with this when he tells us not to pray for God to give a brother life when he commits a sin that leads to death (1 John 5:16-17). Once a name-bear-ing Christian brother commits a capital offense, in or-der to show that his life is characterized by redemption now that he is in our midst, as we have seen, he should be put to death with sufficient witnesses. And if the au-thorities will not allow this, excommunication would satisfy the requirement.

Should God's nation of believers be incapable of judging its own members in every respect? If not, what level of weightiness should we treat as an outside matter?

If a believer steals a lawnmower from another believer, I think everyone would agree that the police should not be involved. That should be dealt with "in-house." In my limited experience, local police would rather most people deal with their own stuff and not call them whenever it's allowed to be handled out of court. Let's say it's something bigger like breaking trust with regard to land ownership? What about a capital offense? Where does Scripture draw a line?

We are commanded to set judges and officials in our towns to judge us (Deuteronomy 16:18). And we are outright forbidden to go law before the ungodly instead of the saints (1 Corinthians 6:1). So should this be pastor/elder/overseers (these titles are all the same role)? Unfortunately most would not be up to the task, much less willing. Yet I don't think the title of the person performing the task is as important as the function. If a pastor/elder/overseer does not want to judge matters that people bring to him, that's fine, but there must be someone who has this responsibility. (Though it is a shame that we as a nation of priests wouldn't know what to do if the local county judge asked us to make a final decision on a case because it's too difficult for him. Why is this not a common occurrence [Deuteronomy

17:8-13]?) If a new role of church judges/scribes/mediators needs to be raised up to perform these duties because pastors/elders/overseers are overwhelmed or didn't sign up for this role, new people need to be trained to fill this role.

The Jews had scribes, judges, and other officials who were assigned to teach and advise on matters of law as well as perform legal tasks like verifying and filing records and documents (marriage contracts, property titles, affidavits, etc.), not to mention making binding decisions. We have the same functions that need to be performed today in the body of Christ. The trouble is that we think of these as secular or godless tasks and responsibilities. Yet the most important thing is that the person doing them be utterly steeped in God's law. Where could someone even get a job as a biblical lawyer or go to be trained as one? We think of scribes and judges in the Bible as being corrupt, and many were (bad lawyers and judges is an old problem), especially in Jesus's day, but Scripture speaks positively of some, particularly Ezra (Ezra 7:6). There is nothing wrong with the role itself; we're commanded to appoint them. But we have largely refused. We need officials and judges desperately.

Now, if someone from outside comes and asks us to hand over someone from within back to them to punish outside, that's another question entirely. We are not allowed to return a slave to his master who escapes to us (Deuteronomy 23:15), but as for murderers or other offenders, each case will need to be handled individually. For these kinds of cases, war is risked for refusal. Going to war to defend slaves who escape to us is perfectly within the realm of acceptability.

Then do we pursue those with the death penalty who flee from the inside? Saul did this before he was called Paul (Acts 26:9-11). If the offenses were committed while inside, I believe this is justified (though of course Saul wasn't in this case because the charges were false.) This would obviously require a lot of extra time, expense, effort, and cooperation from the foreign authorities. Even then, it still may not be feasible. Was the person a professing brother or sister when these things were done? Then that is definitely within our jurisdiction, even if the person has since revoked the name of Christ. They can be cut off or pursued to foreign cities to be put to death. Of course currently our ability to exercise the latter responsibility has been removed, regardless. Excommunication then in practice must be as irreversible as death (apart from Christ) because it is standing in place of execution. Once a brother has been convicted of a capital offense while within the body, there is no option to rejoin the body in this life. He is handed over to Satan for the destruction of his flesh that his soul may be saved (1 Corinthians 5:5).

Why should Christ's body have any authority of execution? Aren't you mixing up the spheres of government? Don't church government and civil government have separate jurisdictions? What about separation of church and state? Building on the answer to the previous objection, this amounts to saying that Israel should have no judges, officials, or magistrates, and that it really only counts if the office is ordained by some secular system.

If there's any separation of powers that Scripture makes clear, it's the separation between priests and non-priests. Believers are priests, and unbelievers are not. We are separate from them. The Greek word used of the assembly of God's people is "ekklesia" or "called-out." We have been called out of the nations to be a new nation. This new nation must have judges and officials. We should be so far above reproach and so skilled at judging ourselves that unbelievers seek us out to decide their cases for them (Deuteronomy 17:8-9, Isaiah 2:2-4, Micah 4:1-5, Zechariah 8:20-23). This is a key sign of healthy kingdom growth in the new covenant. Instead, we are seeking out unbelievers, asking them to put us in office. This is utterly backwards and shameful.

The traditional evangelical spheres of government consist of individual, family, church, and civil. Scripture does not refer to spheres of government. Different realms of jurisdiction have been deduced as generalities, and some of these can be helpful. For example, it is a person's responsibility to provide for the members of his own household (1 Timothy 5:8). If a father decides to provide for his friends at the neglect of his wife and children, he is forgetting his "sphere" of responsibility. Likewise, it is usually his responsibility to discipline his children for disobedience, including use of the rod (Proverbs 13:24). Likewise, if a murderer is caught, it is not an individual's responsibility to execute justice alone. There are requirements that must be followed.

But the spheres do not make sense with many laws. For example, if a son strikes his mother in the presence of sufficient witnesses, his parents are required to bring him before a judge to hear charges for execution. This violation of the law is not dealt with by family government; parents bring it to the city judges. And what if all the witnesses (and therefore some of those required to stone him) were his siblings, or the judge happened to be a brother or uncle? Has the civil government inappropriately descended into the family sphere?

And what is the division between church and civil? Does God's people's realm of authority stop just beneath the level of capital offenses? Are God's people forever required to hand the jurisdiction of the death penalty over to unbelievers? And if not, are God's people supposed to operate by the rules of how unbelieving government systems are set up? Is it not by God's commandments? If believers want to have a role in government, is our only option to wield authority over unbelievers (willing and unwilling alike) using whatever structure happens to be already in place? We are instructed that we are not to judge unwilling unbelievers but to leave them to God (1 Corinthians 5:12-13). We judge ourselves which includes sojourners (willing unbelievers). Israel's jurisdiction ended at its borders. Israel is to judge Israelites and sojourners. Israel was not supposed to try to set up judges and officials in Assyria, Babylon, Egypt, or Rome to make decisions for the other nations. God's design is to draw the nations to Zion willingly (Zechariah 8) as we see pictured with Solomon (1 Kings 10:1-9) through hearing of our wisdom in self judgment (Deuteronomy 4:5-8). We must seek to rule ourselves and serve others. But the human tendency since the fall has been to rule others and serve ourselves. If we rule ourselves well and serve others well, God will give us authority to rule others according to our wisdom, skill, and trustworthiness. We don't have to seek it out for ourselves. See the parable of the talents in Matthew 25:14-30.

Many rightly recognize that civil or city government is an inherently religious task according to Scripture. God has laws for it. If someone disagrees with God's law, he has decided to implement humanistic ideals as the basis for city government. This replaces God's laws with a false god's laws—man's. This is the idolatry of humanism.

So are God's people supposed to have their own court systems with judges capable of hearing every kind of accusation? If not, the alternative would mean that believers are only supposed to handle small matters, but important things are left to unbelievers to judge for us. But we know that believers are forbidden to take matters between believers to be judged by unbelievers under any circumstance (1 Corinthians 6:1-7). This would be like an Israelite dragging another Israelite to Assyria or Rome for judgment. Could you imagine Solomon traveling abroad to the Queen of Sheba to ask her advice? "Do you not know that we are to judge angels? How much more, then, matters pertaining to this life!" (1 Corinthians 6:3). A capital offense pales in comparison to the matters we will one day judge for angels. Scripture emphatically says we are meant to judge all matters of this life. Is a capital offense not a matter of this life? Israel is supposed to have its own judges and officials for everything, including capital offenses (Deuteronomy 16:18). We are not meant to rely on foreign nations for our courts for any kind of case. We should not be content that our only practical option is to call the city or state police to take our capital offenders for judgment. If that's our only option, it's God's judgment for our failure to obey God in our own courts (if we even have any as believers).

While this may scare some unbelievers, it should give them comfort. Believers have no jurisdiction judging unbelievers (like how many people think of Islam implementing sharia law). God judges outsiders (1 Corinthians 5:13). Why should we step into a role God has reserved for Himself alone? A believer may find himself in this position and even rule in a godly manner, but if not gained by God's design as fruit of service to others, it will not be held for long. Believers are to judge themselves, and then the nations will be drawn in to God when they see the fruit. The reason so many are repelled is because we reject God's wisdom. This has attracted lawless people to take God's name upon themselves in vain. This is a heavenly trademark violation, as it were. God's name is his trademark. This is representing God with a wrong example. If we reject God's law because we are embarrassed by it, we will be ridiculed. We are rightly called inconsistent Christians who are in denial. Instead of repenting, we deny the application of God's law even more fervently. This leads to even more ridicule in a vicious cycle.

The two simultaneous objections to my position will then become:

1. "Christians should be involved in government." To which I would respond:

2. Over believers and sojourners, yes, we should be. Over unwilling unbelievers, no, we should not be.

and

1. "God's people should have no authority of execution." To which I would respond:

2. Over believers and sojourners, yes, we should have it. Over unwilling unbelievers, no, we should not have it.

This would preclude us from running for office over outsiders generally, if not in every case, and certainly not as a standard strategy.

Galatians 6:7-10 is a key reminder: "Do not be deceived: God is not mocked, for whatever one sows, that will he also reap. For the one who sows to his own flesh will from the flesh reap corruption, but the one who sows to the Spirit will from the Spirit reap eternal life. And let us not grow weary of doing good, for in due season we will reap, if we do not give up. So then, as we have opportunity, let us do good to everyone, and especially to those who are of the household of faith."

As difficult as it is for a believer to select a church judge when he has an important dispute with another believer (churches are notoriously bad at handling conflict resolution, much less training others to do it), how would that same believer like it if an unbeliever got a say in who his church judge is? If we don't want to be treated like this, we should not treat unbelievers this way. We reap what we sow.

This diagram is an ultimate one. It does not mean that the obedient will not face tests and persecution in the short run.

OUR ACTIONS   GOD'S RESPONSE

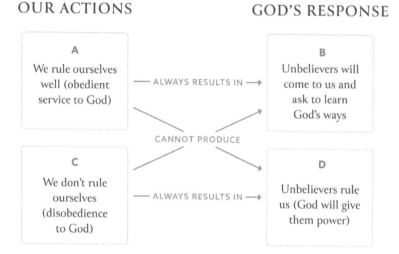

There are four theoretical options:

1. **C and D:** While this is a natural progression, it will draw disdain from unbelievers and make us their slaves. At least in admitting this option Christians aren't being hypocrites.

2. **A and D:** While this option is technically impossible, in my experience it's the most widely held position by believers in America. This is a slightly less dangerous position than C and B but still bad. This position will attract those

who are already believers, but unbelieving opposition will grow to match it. Proportionally speaking, no ground will ever be gained for Christ. This thinking is a result of the self-fulfilling belief that the world will become increasingly sinful before Christ's return. This position neglects a key parable of Christ describing His kingdom that His return will require a long wait (Matthew 25:1-13). Unbelievers asking to be ruled by us is prophesied as a key sign of the new covenant (Zechariah 8:20-23).

3. **C and B:** This position is characterized by trying to gain power over unbelievers the same way they attempt to gain power over one another (Matthew 20:25-27). This includes seeking authority over them directly. Unbelievers are more skilled in this than we can ever be, and God will oppose them in the end anyway. This is a position many believers attempt to practice even if they would argue otherwise. This makes Christians worse than irrelevant to unbelievers; it makes Christians cancerous enemies to be actively opposed by unbelievers. And it will result in D anyway, however dedicated the attempt is. God will personally arm and strengthen the unbelievers against us as far as we fail to rule ourselves well.

4. **A and B:** This is the correct combination.
    Unbelievers will be drawn to us and help us glad-
    ly when we bear good fruit by faith in Christ.
    Counter-intuitively, when we govern ourselves
    well, God will give us authority to govern unbe-
    lievers. We don't even need to seek it. The same
    way a tree draws water upward, unbelievers will
    flow up to the city on a hill. I call this "Zero-
    Compromise Incrementalism."

There is a disconnect here that runs deep. God's people are to judge themselves and willing sojourners *and no
one else* rightly in all matters. *God will judge everyone else*
(1 Corinthians 5:12-13). If believers have no authority
of execution, then no believer can ever serve as a witness in a capital case, for the witnesses must cast the first
stones, and the people must follow suit. By God's design,
the earthly judge does not execute; he's not participating as a witness. This eliminates the objection that the
church does not "bear the sword." Technically speaking, the sword is only used for inter-city offenses, name-
ly war. But as it is used in Romans 13:4, "the sword" is
symbolic of all punishment for evildoing. This pushes
the question back to Romans 13:1: who is the governing
authority who bears the sword? The governing authority is whoever is set in place by God. The more important question is: who *should* be the governing authority

in a believer's life? It ideally should never be unbelievers bearing the sword over us, because God only allows that when we are disobedient. The only reason we think of this as normal is because we've been under judgment for so long that we don't remember that freedom in this jurisdiction even exists. The only time God puts the ungodly in authority is either when we ask for it or when there is no one godly who is as qualified. Shame on us! Do we as believers want to be ruled by the ungodly or the godly? We will be ruled in all matters in one way or another. Refusing to choose to be governed by God's commandments is choosing to be governed by the ungodly.

If we then wish to be ruled by the godly, should we seek power over unbelievers the same way unbelievers seek power?—by trying to assert power over those outside our jurisdiction? Israel's jurisdiction includes those who are within the borders of spiritual Israel—those who bear Christ's name. Extra-territorial judicial action against another nation should rightly be seen as committing an offense against God. God judges unbelievers, and we should not encroach on His sole jurisdiction. Moreover, why should we seek to govern unbelievers while our own house is in such neglect? Unbelievers rightly scorn us in this area according to 1 Timothy 3:4-5.

As much as the Pharisees and Jewish religious leaders hated Moses and the law, they still at least had a correct desire to govern themselves within their proper jurisdiction, even though their governing was corrupt. The Jews had enough favor with the Roman authorities to be granted jurisdiction in Acts 18:12-17 when Gallio refused to judge on religious matters between the Jews and Paul. Gallio left it up to the Jews to beat Sosthenes, and he paid no attention. While this was of course un-just on the Jews' part, it shows a proper understanding that a Jew was part of Israel and therefore under their jurisdiction, even while under subjugation in a Roman province outside of the physical territory of Israel. This is supposed to be done because Deuteronomy 13:12-18 is always in view, and letting things progress to that level is utterly terrifying. It is important to nip a false gospel in the bud. In that much, they were right.

God commands us to set judges and officials over ourselves in all our towns (Deuteronomy 16:18). Just as priests are representatives, so are judges in a sense. And if the judges can't work out a matter, the priests are there to handle judges' requests for decisions. So even within Israel itself, there is a picture of believers and unbeliev-ers. The priests (believers) are a subset of Israel among the non-priestly tribes (unbelievers). The most difficult matters are to be brought by a judge to the priests to determine, and there is no higher level of appeal as far as the physical world is concerned. Anyone who disre-garded the ruling of a case that was appealed by a judge to a priest was to be put to death (Deuteronomy 17:8-13).

When we become believers, we become citizens of the heavenly kingdom (Philippians 3:20). This does not necessarily undo whatever earthly citizenship we have. Paul used his Roman citizenship strategically in further-ance of the gospel on multiple occasions (Acts 16:37-38, 22:25-28, 25:11-12). He also counted this Roman citi-zenship as dung compared to his heavenly citizenship (Philippians 3:8). Some people payed large amounts of money to gain Roman citizenship (Acts 22:28). Why does Paul speak in such seemingly contradictory ways? What good is a heavenly citizenship on earth or an earthly citizenship in heaven?

We should submit to earthly rulers (without sin) as to God, and because of our new citizenship, we must submit to our heavenly ruler, Christ, even more-so. A primary way we must display this citizenship to unbe-lievers is how we "go to law" (to use Scripture's phrase) when we have a dispute with one another. We are meant to choose righteous judges for ourselves in every city (Deuteronomy 16:18) rather than having God or other men pick our judges for us.

Under the Aaronic priesthood, the priests did not have any land as an inheritance. They had cities spread like salt throughout Israel. Likewise as believers who are priests, our inheritance is in the new earth, not this one, and we are also the salt of the earth. One of the ways we salt the earth is by being spread throughout the unbelievers to season them to God's taste. Justice and lawful mercy (in and out of court) is this seasoning.

Within our jurisdiction, Scripture is clear—believers may not ever take a matter involving only believers to be heard by unbelievers. Period. This is like Jewish judges appealing to Egyptian judges. "When one of you has a grievance against another, does he dare go to law before the unrighteous instead of the saints?" (1 Corinthians 6:1). This includes capital offenses—everything. We are rather to be wronged and defrauded than do so because we will judge angels (verses 3 and 7). Unbelievers are supposed to appeal to us (Micah 4:1-5), not have us seeking them out because we can't handle our own affairs.

CHAPTER 9

So What Should I Do?

The bulk of this chapter has been redacted for strategic purposes. To see if you are eligible to purchase this complete chapter, visit voluntarytheocracy.org/stoning

THE MOST ANALOGOUS SITUATION on this topic to the present day is the Babylonian captivity. The book of Jeremiah details the events leading up to the captivity and the beginning of the captivity itself. Daniel and Ezekiel were written during this captivity, and then Ezra and Nehemiah detail the return to Jerusalem and the rebuilding of the city walls by the Jewish remnant.

Just before the captivity, Jewish prophets were giving false prophecies that they would not be captured and taken by the king of Babylon (Jeremiah 27:9-17). And then shortly after they were taken captive, the prophets continued prophesying that the exiles would be freed from captivity within two years (28:1-4). God killed the prophet who spoke this in opposition to Jeremiah's prophecy (28:16-17). This is like people today who are saying that our return to the heavenly Jerusalem is coming soon. God told the people that it was going to be generations, 70 years of captivity in Babylonia (Jeremiah 25:11). He told them they should build houses, plant gardens and eat their produce, take wives and have sons and daughters, and seek the welfare of Babylon and pray for it (Jeremiah 29:4-14). In other words, you will be free and blessed in the future, but it's going to be a while. This is a common pattern in Scripture. Remember how most of the Hebrews died in the wilderness before their children could enter the promised land. They had to wander and die in the wilderness for not trusting God. So be faithful in the meantime where you can today. We're in the same situation with capital offenses.

The Jews did seek the good of Babylon as unto the Lord as detailed in the book of Daniel. This service to the king of Babylon involved disobedience to him at times. We see the account of the rescue from the firey furnace when Hananiah, Mishael, and Azariah (Shadrach,

Meshach, and Abednego) ignored Nebuchadnezzar's decree ordering them to commit idolatry (Daniel 3). We see the account of Daniel praying to God in public when Darius ordered anyone who prayed other than to himself to be thrown into the lions' den (Daniel 6). In both of these cases, God miraculously saved those who obeyed God rather than the king of Babylon or Persia.

After 70 years of faithfully serving Babylon in repentance, and after God punished Babylon itself with its own Persian conquerors (Daniel 5:28), the Jews had built up such a reputation of obedience to God that Ezra was granted full authority by Artaxerxes I king of Persia to return to Jerusalem and reinstate their authority of setting up officials and capital punishment there, stated in the manner of one who does not know God's law (Ezra 7:25-26).

This is our pattern to follow. We have had the authority to put our members to death taken from us by God for our rebellion to His law. It is good that it has been stripped away from us by the nations at this time. The church has rejected this responsibility and engaged in all kinds of capital offenses to boot. We have not proven ourselves ready to be trusted with it again yet. Church jurisdiction over capital offenses sounds scary. It is certainly a weighty responsibility. We are under-qualified because we have been actively rejecting this responsibility and handing it over to unbelievers. Who wants an ignorant and rebellious judge (ignorant *because* he is rebellious) to decide whether someone lives or dies? I shudder to think how much worse of a name Christ would have among unbelievers if we had this authority right now. We get it back by seeking the good of the city and serving Nebuchadnezzar, as it were, as unto the Lord without sin. This will show a spirit of repentance. This will include civil disobedience at times as with Daniel and the Hebrew midwives (Exodus 1:15-21). But if it is in obedience to God, he will save us from the furnaces and lions' dens, as it were. By doing this, we will have a good name restored to us, as Nebuchadnezzar praised the Jews for setting aside his own decrees in obedience to God (Daniel 3:28-30). This good name takes generations to build, and the work can be undone quickly. Each person will have a slightly different role to play in the details of daily life, but there are a few overarching steps that everyone should take:

1. Change your opinion on public stoning and understand it as lawful and ideal. If people don't agree that public stoning is just, it will not happen. This is not a negative but a requirement of the stoning laws themselves. Stoning can only exist where it is understood to be righteous and practiced lawfully by all the people because the witnesses and congregation must carry it out.

Otherwise no testimony can be brought forward to begin with. If we fail to trust Moses, how can we trust Christ (John 5:46)? The consequence is that we will have responsibility stripped from us as it is now and as it happened under the lawless rule of the Pharisees and subsequent Assyrian, Babylonian, and Roman subjugations. We will bear the consequences until we repent according to the spirit of the law by the power of the Holy Spirit.

2. Take every law requiring the death penalty and flip it around as a positive command. Simple examples: Honor your parents. Teach your children to honor you. Treat God's name as holy in your speech and actions. Damning someone is blasphemy for a man to say, for only God has this authority (Mark 2:7), therefore practice rebuking in love and taking every opportunity to encourage one another.

3. If you are an elder, lay this before congregations in your city and make these expectations widely understood as the most basic code of conduct. Once this primary circle is taught, find those who would most benefit from learning it for the first time and teach them (prisoners, broken homes, victims of capital offenses, etc.)

4. Discuss this topic with your circles and take action where you have the freedom to immediately as they become feasible. If you won't take action where you can now, you will stay in Babylon when given the opportunity to return to Jerusalem, and your heritage will be forfeited.

5. Create and publish a public record of all who continue to claim Christ's name in your city after excommunication. 1 Corinthians 5:11 says if anyone who has been cut off persists in claiming Christ's name, we are not even allowed to eat with such a person. 2 John 1:10-11 says we may not greet him or allow him into a believer's house. And if he ceases being called by Christ's name, he cannot take it back up again (Hebrews 6:6). So there must be permanent, public records of these things. We must purify ourselves from their influence and not inadvertently tarnish ourselves. Christ's body is being defiled by "filthy Christians," because they blur the battle lines. They need to be publicly identified and publicly cut off (either by death or irrevocable excommunication). They are subverting the cause of Christ. They're the ones we must be on guard against. Unbelievers are much less dangerous. They are clear what side of the war they're on,

and they pose no threat to us as long as we remain faithful to God.

6. If you would like to meet other believers who are also searching for this radical form of accountability (an essential foundation for any nation) to discuss it and learn more about it, submit an application to the Voluntary Theocracy Database at voluntarytheocracy.org/stoning.

7. Commit with your nearby fellow believers to hold one another accountable under pain of death (public and permanent excommunication for the time being) and set a trustworthy member of your group who follows justice to hear disputes with one another (Deuteronomy 16:18). But first, you will have to frequently discuss God's law with one another to arrive at this deep level of trust. An hour every Sunday with one man addressing fifty won't accomplish this in a generation of Sundays (much less addressing five hundred or ten thousand). If someone refuses to submit to discipline with two or three witnesses, cut him off. Do not associate with him, greet him, or eat with him ever again until he submits. If he submits, and once this authority has been regained, put him to death. Needless lives are being lost for failing to do this. True community and

God's favor and protection (to grant us either favor with the unbelieving authorities or protection from them) are prerequisites for pursuing this step completely.

CHAPTER 10

Practical Objections

If there's a truthful single eyewitness of a murder and substantial accompanying evidence, can't courts today do an excellent job of determining the facts of a case with modern DNA evidence and similar techniques?

Before public stoning (or any other requirement enforced by a court) can be practiced lawfully in a city, the people in that city must understand that a judge can't hear a case without two witnesses accusing who would be punished accordingly if found to be lying. Without two witnesses at least, even a murderer must not be punished in any way. After seriously contemplating the ramifications of this, most people would be uncomfortable with this high standard as being too risky to public safety. Someone could see a murder and call the authorities who give a public adjuration for other witnesses to come forward and testify (Leviticus 5:1). And if no one else comes forward, nothing should be done, even though all common sense points directly to the guilty man. Even if this objection would not often be verbalized first, it would likely be the first practical problem that people would have as a stepping stone to handling capital offenses properly in a Biblical system. DNA and other evidences could be used, but Leviticus 5:1 also defines a witness as someone who comes to know a matter. Evidence must be interpreted. If an expert is willing to back up his findings with his life, he could be admitted as a second witness, but this standard is not currently applied to expert testimony today as it should be.

Won't unbelievers charge us with murder or taking the law into our own hands?

We don't seek to stone outsiders (non-Israelites / non-believers / non-sojourners)—that's not within our jurisdiction. What do we have to do with judging outsiders? God will judge them (1 Corinthians 5:12-13). We only want to judge ourselves and willing sojourners among us who choose to live by these standards also. So is this voluntarily agreeing to be stoned? Yes. Shouldn't a murderer admit what he did and face the consequences in honesty? So if unbelievers think this is crazy, why would they stop us from enforcing this on ourselves? "They'll eradicate themselves and make themselves a stench to repel new people." Right?

Therefore the only reasonable reason that unbelievers would try to stop believers from enforcing this on ourselves is because they're afraid that it might actually be beneficial to believers and produce earth-changing results for the better of mankind. By opposing us in this, they would give this idea credibility. And by supporting us, they help us. Either they discredit themselves, or we win. They must choose. Read Zechariah 8:20-23. This is in our future. I ask them which team they would like to be on. Unbelievers will grab Christians by the sleeve in the street and ask to come along with us. If we obey God, the world will see the fruit and be drawn to us. We don't need to chase them down. We preach to people to come and pick fruit from a bare orchard and wonder why no one comes. We need to begin growing fruit, and when there is fruit ready on the trees, we won't need to worry about not being able to draw enough people.

Imagine the message we would send to the world with this situation: a believer has confessed and subsequently been found guilty of a capital offense in the body of believers. The man knew the consequences of his action and came forward willingly to accept the death penalty, which the witnesses and the people in the body carry out. Imagine how unbelievers would respond. What steps need to be taken to draw men into a community like this where they know these standards in advance?

If we build this kind of community, and the world wants to attack us for it, may God judge between us and the unbelievers. I think we'll withstand anything they can hit us with at that stage.

Isn't stoning barbaric?

I believe our primary concern should be over whether or not something is right. I also think this whole discussion is over the very definition of what barbaric or uncivilized means. The question is: who gets to decide what the law is? In one sense, yes, stoning is barbaric and violent. God's design is that a man reaps what he sows. Sowing barbarity reaps barbarity, and the whole population is supposed to be taught that in a graphic way to steer them away from barbarity. What is barbarity, and by what standard? Is a capital offense not barbarity? Stoning is supposed to give a lawless and barbaric people an objective look at the consequences of their actions and give them an opportunity to change and prevent themselves from doing evil. This will produce a lawful, civilized, and productive city free of barbarism.

Are you not dreaming of a utopia?

Yes, and Scripture loves telling us about it and encourages us to look forward to it and work towards it: Jeremiah 31:31-40, 33:14-26, Psalm 110, Isaiah 2:1-4, 29:17-19, 32:15-18, 35:3-6, 60:15-18, 61:1-2, Zephaniah 3:9-20, Hosea 2:20-22, Amos 9:13-15, Micah 4:1-8, Hebrews 8:8-10, Zechariah 8:20-23, 14:1-21.

Will the rulers of the nations ever even let us?

This objection is not a problem with the argument's validity or invalidity, but it brings up the main topic of discussion I had hoped that this book would spark. We must seek diligently to govern ourselves in these extreme yet fundamental areas while we learn and remain to be faithful in the little things in the meantime. The first congregation that actually stones a believer to death will send a message around the world, and we must be fully prepared to give an answer to the world in the spirit of repentance. I intend for this book to be one such resource. Before that happens, God's people must build up a strong defense in the Lord from such an attack. We must root ourselves deeply in helping the poor as unto the Lord.

Artaxerxes I willingly granted this authority back to God's people in Ezra 7:26. They had served Babylon and Persia faithfully for 70 years, and so God granted them favor with the ruler of the day who saw their

righteous conduct and encouraged them to execute offenders among their people and teach the ways of God
to everyone who didn't know them. We should seek the
same favor with those in power today without sinning
in gaining their favor.

If someone suffers unjustly for doing what is right,
this is seen as a gracious thing in God's eyes (1 Peter
2:18-19). The question remains: if the people solve their
own affairs properly through the correct means, why
should our authorities be unhappy? Can anyone remain
in authority long who punishes good and rewards evil
(Romans 13:3-4)? Not by divine standards.

This is a long-term goal, and it must be done strategically and with great wisdom and caution. Otherwise, the
ground we gain in this area can be undone, we will have
to start over, and the next attempt will be that much
more difficult.

The Hebrew midwives didn't ask permission to obey
God. They lied to pharaoh about their obedience to
God, and God consequently blessed them with families (Exodus 1:15-21). They sowed life and reaped life.
I can hear some thinking, "But the midwives did it to
save lives. Stoning only takes life. That's not sowing
life." While this appears to be the case at first, it's not
true by God's design. Remember, the fundamental reason for stoning is "that all the people may hear and fear
and never do such a thing among you again." By causing

people to fear God, a single stoning will save many more lives that would otherwise be lost. An ounce of prevention is worth a pound of cure.

Living as a believer in the United States of America in the early third millennium, I know there are many fruits of obedience to Christ that I haven't tasted. There are many fruits that I have never seen, and there are many, many more that I don't know exist. Imagine a community with interest-free loans between believers, loans which are completely forgiven if not repaid within six years. Some families would have restored a thief to his full status of innocence via Biblically lawful slavery. They would have given him a solid education in work ethics.

There would be no prisons, because the system of justice and restoration would be swift and effective. Dealing with a few capital cases would instill fear of wrongdoing in a city so that it is not attempted again for years or generations. Children given over to serious rebellion or rampant drug abuse would be spoken of publicly with fear, and such parents would learn the devastating consequences of children in rebellion. All children would have a knowledge of the tremendous rewards for honoring their parents and the devastating consequences for ultimately rejecting their instruction.

We must build strong communities by truly sharing with one another, freely lending to brothers, being regularly hospitable to strangers and those who hate us. We must see foreign people, the poor, the widow, orphan, and fatherless as opportunities to give our tithes to them (Deuteronomy 14:28-29) and make God known. We need to apply these principles to show that the rewards and blessings in the next life are worth far more than the basic punishments of restitution and execution in this life.

We must realize that God holds us responsible if the nations despise Him because of our representative behavior toward Him and others (Romans 2:24).

As Zechariah 8:20-23 says, the nations will seek us out and grab us by the sleeves to ask us if they may accompany us to entreat God. We will not force them to have such a desire, but their hearts will be drawn in when they see our good works and glorify God, as Christ has told us (Matthew 7:15-19, Deuteronomy 4:5-8). Sexual immorality and covetousness would not even be named among us (Ephesians 5:3).

If our focus turns to obeying God in the most neglected areas, He will again fight for us, and no nation can stop us from our obedience. Turn to God, for He is our refuge. Turning to God means turning away from our impurity. We must cleanse ourselves. Be strong and courageous.

Won't this draw disdain and ridicule?

First, while is it important to be thought well of by outsiders (1 Peter 2:12), and favor with them will certainly be one fruit of obedience to God, the short-term opinion of outsiders is not the ultimate standard by which we must conduct ourselves. And even if it were, I believe it will draw ridicule and scorn from those who show themselves unfit for the gospel. For it is God's law that brings knowledge of sin. And anyone who denies that he is a sinner will see no need of a savior, and the law teaches us what sin is (Romans 7:7). I do not believe this will draw ridicule from those who have been chosen by God. Ridicule from unbelievers who are wrong is a good thing. This allows all to see their unreasonableness. This may bring Scriptural challenges and criticism from believers, which is good, but it will not bring ridicule from them. In the end, if I am correct, it will not ultimately bring dishonor on us (Deuteronomy 4:5-8). It will actually bring us honor and favor with the nations (Zechariah 8:20-23). And we know the gospel will be victorious (Isaiah 2:1-4). The law paves the way for the gospel, for the law lifts the valleys, makes the mountains low, and straightens crooked paths (Isaiah 40:4, 45:2). The gospel is news of equity and freedom—difficult for the rich, but joyous news to the poor and brokenhearted.

If you have read from the beginning to here and are still not onboard with public stoning, maybe I can summarize what's going on in your heart:

1. "I believe the words of Moses (John 5:46-47), and I know that Jesus condemned the Pharisees for

nullifying Moses even when it came to stoning children (Mark 7:9-13)."

2.   "Yes, I agree that the law is good (1 Timothy 1:8)."

3.   "I know that anyone who has died to the law has been made alive to righteousness by faith, and if I rebuild what I tore down, I'm a transgressor of the law (Romans 6:11, Galatians 2:18-19)."

4.   "And I know that Jesus said heaven and earth will pass away before the law passes away, and whoever nullifies the commandments will be considered least in God's kingdom (Matthew 5:17-19)."

5.   "Yes, the law is eternal, and I died to the law in Christ (Psalm 119:160, Romans 6:8)."

6.   "I know that we shouldn't nullify the law but that we establish the law by our faith (Romans 3:31)."

7.   "And I think the laws about the death penalty are good, but I don't think I should be involved in executing someone myself, and definitely not as a member of the body of Christ."

No one can drag you kicking and screaming to accept this. And unless I am wrong on one or several underlying conclusions that this position is based on, 1-6 will push you strongly toward something close to this position as well. Our goal as believers is supposed to be one of bearing fruit. Instead, point 7 evidences a lack of trust in God's word. When God instructs me to do something that is uncomfortable and counter-cultural, I should not go looking for ways out of my responsibility before Him. Our spirit must be one of obedience first and understanding second as little children. Too often we refuse to obey the Father's voice because we don't understand His commandments, and we don't understand them because we're not focused on doing them. It is a vicious cycle. We should certainly understand the spirit behind the commandments, but even if we don't, we must trust and obey anyway to learn about the spirit. We don't see Christ in capital punishment because we are unwilling to hold ourselves accountable to the law in faith. When we refuse to obey, Christ will not show Himself to us (John 14:21). Is it therefore any wonder that so many don't see Christ in it?

Nevertheless, if you are still in disagreement, I encourage you to voice your opposition to these conclusions with a strong foundation in Scripture. In doing so, you must also present an ideal alternative system for church discipline for repentant capital offenders, and you may not involve unbelievers in making these decisions or carrying out the penalties according to 1 Corinthians 6:1-8. This commandment from Paul is given immediately following his judgment against a capital offender in chapter 5.

CHAPTER 11

Further Concepts

Burning

There are two sins which are placed in a special category highlighted by burning. One applies only to women,
and one to men and women both. The punishment for
women is when the daughter of a priest has sex outside
of marriage, either before or after she has a husband
(Leviticus 21:9). There is also a death penalty for the
Israelite daughter of a non-priest, but in that circumstance, she is to be stoned, either on her father's door-
step if it was before marriage (Deuteronomy 22:13-21), or
just a regular stoning if it was adultery (Leviticus 20:10).

The punishment for men and women both is when
a man marries both a woman and her mother. In this

situation, the man and both women are to be burned with fire (Leviticus 20:14).

Leviticus 13:47-59 lists laws for burning infected articles made of cloth or skin. Things have to be burned when there is no hope of cleansing something or making it fruitful, and it has the power to spread (Hebrews 6:4-8). For houses that have a persistent disease that can't be cleansed, they have to be torn down stone by stone and timber by timber (Leviticus 14:33-57). This is what happened to the temple (Matthew 24:2, Mark 13:2, Luke 21:6). The temple was torn down and burned in 70 AD, signifying the irredeemable fruitlessness of Israel's rejection of the Messiah.

For those who are destined for hell, there is no hope of forgiveness, for even though they have been purchased by Christ, they continue in their rebellion (2 Peter 2:1). When Christ purchased them, He was given authority to cast them into hell forever.

For these two offenses, there is no quenching the fire that has been kindled. These penalties are a shadow of the lake of fire.

Cut off

Exodus 31:14 seems to equivocate cutting someone off from his people with putting someone to death. This would certainly make sense as to why only the twelve followed Jesus in John 6:52-69. Jesus was asking those

who followed Him in drinking His blood to be willing
to die His death after Him. If Jesus wanted to undo or
clarify the idea that drinking blood would be worthy of
being cut off, this moment definitely would have been
the opportune time to do so when it kept so many from
following Him. Yet He purposefully gave them a hard
saying and let their understanding persist to separate the
twelve from the rest of His disciples.

The purpose of stoning or cutting someone off is that
God's people may purge themselves of evil to be pure
in service to Him. Removing someone from association
and refusing to eat with him both accomplish this. This
is why Paul hands the unrepentant over to Satan (1
Corinthians 5:11, 1 Timothy 1:20), and God will judge
him as being outside the body (1 Corinthians 5:12-13).

There is an argument to be made that someone can't
decide to switch what jurisdiction his capital offense
took place in. That's where he is to be judged. In this
case, being excommunicated is not the ideal, but it is a
functional solution where we have no authority to judge
capital offenses within the church with execution. This
may be the reason for its practice in the early church.

Cherem/the ban/devoted

There is one category of death penalty that is even more
serious than burning alone. The ban is also known as

being "devoted to the Lord," and sometimes it's referred to by the Hebrew word "cherem." The ban requires two forms of execution, either stoning and burning for individuals (Joshua 7:25), or if it's an entire city to be devoted, putting every breathing thing in it to the sword, and burning everything (Deuteronomy 13:12-18). Fire is always involved since being devoted under the ban is for the purpose of being a burnt offering (verse 16).

Offerings must be holy, and there are degrees of holiness illustrated in the temple. There was the court of the nations, the court of women, the court of Israel, the court of priests, and the holy of holies, where only the high priest could enter on the day of atonement. Anyone who entered a place beyond that person's status was to be put to death. God would kill anyone directly who violated the holy of holies, with men required to enforce death in the lower courts.

The ban is only mentioned a handful of times in the law. From these, we can gain a complete picture of how the ban works. Anything under the ban could not have a substitution for it (Leviticus 27:29). The same was true for anyone who sheds blood, even if the person did not fall under the ban (Numbers 35:33), for anyone who makes a vow to be paid by offering an animal (Leviticus 27:9-10), or for the tithe of animals (Leviticus 27:32-33). For the last two examples with animals, any attempt to purchase back what had been made holy would result in the substitution becoming holy as well. In trying to save or ransom things in this case, more is lost. It's a point of no return. Think of trying to pick up a piece of paper from beneath lava. The paper is already gone, and when you pull your arm back, so is your hand. So the same principle is true with the ban and with shedding blood, nonredeemable. The same is true for a garment that has leprosy (Leviticus 13:47-52). It can't be cleansed.

The list of offenses for this is short:

1. "Whoever sacrifices to any god, other than the Lord alone, shall be devoted" (Exodus 22:20).

2. "The carved images of their gods [Hittites, Girgashites, Amorites, Canaanites, Perizzites, Hivites, and Jebusites] you shall burn with fire. You shall not covet the silver or the gold that is on them or take it for yourselves, lest you be ensnared by it, for it is an abomination to the Lord your God. And you shall not bring an abominable thing into your house and become devoted devoted like it. You shall utterly detest and abhor it, for it is devoted" (Deuteronomy 7:25-26).

3. "If you hear in one of your cities, which the Lord your God is giving you to dwell there, that certain worthless fellows have gone out among you and have drawn away the inhabitants of their city,

saying, 'Let us go and serve other gods,' which
you have not known, then you shall inquire and
make search and ask diligently. And behold, if it
be true and certain that such an abomination has
been done among you, you shall surely put the
inhabitants of that city to the sword, devoting all
who are in it and its cattle, with the edge of the
sword. You shall gather all its spoil into the midst
of its open square and burn the city and all its
spoil with fire, as a whole burnt offering to the
Lord your God. It shall be a heap forever. It shall
not be built again. None of the devoted things
shall stick to your hand, that the Lord may turn
from the fierceness of his anger and show you
mercy and have compassion on you and multi-
ply you, as he swore to your fathers, if you obey
the voice of the Lord your God, keeping all his
commandments that I am commanding you today, and doing what is right in the sight of the
Lord your God" (Deuteronomy 13:12-18).

4. "But in the cities of these peoples that the Lord
    your God is giving you for an inheritance, you
    shall save alive nothing that breathes, but you
    shall devote devote [sic] the Hittites and the
    Amorites, the Canaanites and the Perizzites, the
    Hivites and the Jebusites, as the Lord your God

has commanded, that they may not teach you to do according to all their abominable practices that they have done for their gods, and so you sin against the Lord your God." (Deuteronomy 20:16-18).

Being put under the ban is always related to idolatry and whoring after other gods. The Israelites failed to devote all the Canaanites due to their idolatry (Judges 1:27-36). So Israel continued to struggle with idolatry spread to them by the Canaanites. Anything put under the ban spreads if not burned, just like a leprous garment (Leviticus 13:52).

This raises the question: if the ban and murder specify capital offenses that can't have substitution made, does that mean other capital offenses can be substituted? For example, can someone else be put to death to satisfy the penalty for a blasphemer? Christ certainly has this authority, and there is at least one capital offense in Scripture that would seem to be in favor of this:

"When an ox gores a man or a woman to death, the ox shall be stoned, and its flesh shall not be eaten, but the owner of the ox shall not be liable. But if the ox has been accustomed to gore in the past, and its owner has been warned but has not kept it in, and it kills a man or a woman, the ox shall be stoned, and its owner also shall be put to death. If a ransom is imposed on him, then he shall give for the redemption of his life whatever is imposed on him" (Exodus 21:28-30).

In this one case of negligence, the man indirectly responsible for the death of a freeman can pay to save his life if the judge or accusers decide to grant that option. A murderer has no such option. What about other capital offenses? It is possible that when Scripture uses the phrase "dying he shall die," or "stoning he shall be stoned" often translated "surely put to death," or "surely be stoned" that this means the offense is not able to be ransomed. That discussion is necessary, but it is beyond the scope of this book.

Remove from the altar

There is a curious phrase used only once in Scripture. "Whoever strikes a man so that he dies shall be put to death. But if he did not lie in wait for him, but God let him fall into his hand, then I will appoint for you a place to which he may flee. But if a man willfully attacks another to kill him by cunning, you shall take him from my altar, that he may die" (Exodus 21:12-14).

It says that a murderer is to be removed from the Lord's altar so that he may die. It's curious because we typically think of things being put on the altar to be burned up. Yet in this example, a murderer is taken from the altar so that he dies. When considered in conjunction that in order for Christ to be raised again to life in us, he had to offer it on the altar and die there. So while being taken off the altar seems like a mercy, it's actually a serious condemnation. The altar was not a "got to" but a "get to." God set up boundaries around the altar so that not just anyone had access to it. Anyone cut off from the Lord's altar had no hope of making offerings. The horns of the altar (its strength) were considered a place of refuge. See 1 Kings 1:50-53, 2:28-34, and Amos 3:13-15.

No hand shall touch him

In Exodus 19:13 if someone touched Mount Sinai, God commanded that person to be stoned or shot, and no hand shall touch him. We are not told why no hand shall touch him. This could refer to not needing to take him to a judge. In other words, he dies on the spot. And what if someone touches him? Does that second man become worthy of death? We know that God's holiness brings destruction to unholy things. Profane things usually spread their uncleanness to anything they touch. God's holiness in the old covenant destroys unclean things, so it can't spread. Ezekiel 44:19 warns the priests not to spread holiness to the people with their priestly garments. In the new covenant, however, holiness is "contagious" and cleanses whatever it comes into contact with (Matthew 8:1-4, 9:20-22, 26). Anything that cannot be cleansed must be burned with fire (Leviticus 13:47-52).

In Leviticus 24:14, we find an account of a man who blasphemed. God instructs the people who heard him to lay their hands on his head. Was it because they had to repeat the blasphemy in order to bear witness against him, and this signified that they were putting the guilt back on him? Regardless, it reminds us of offerings in the temple when the priest lays his hand on the offering. There's something different about the mountain. It seems as if for a blasphemer, his guilt passed around to everyone who heard, and so the people had to lay their hands on him to signify that their guilt was being placed back on to the one who blasphemed. With touching the mountain, no such guilt seems to have passed to those who saw him do it. He only dies for his own sin since no hand is laid on him.

Capital confession

In 2 Samuel 1:1-16, a man confesses to killing king Saul. David called to a young man to kill him immediately. I do not believe David was right in this judgment. Firstly, because we know the man lied. Saul killed himself (1 Samuel 31:3-6). The man who confessed to killing Saul thought he would gain favor with David for having killed the previous king. Secondly, I do not believe confession of a single witness is an exception to the law requiring two or three witnesses. Scripture does not mention it. A confession against oneself would have to be accompanied by one or two other eyewitnesses for a total of two or three. It would require the confessor to cast a stone at himself, which would be highly unusual for sure, but not impossible.

This would dissuade taking the blame for someone else's capital offense. (We must exhibit this behavior for lesser offenses, but in matters of life and death, only God can make substitution.) This ensures that there is always at least one person testifying who tells the truth because his life depends on it.

Spiritual versus physical

In the beginning, God made a perfect world, a shadow of heaven. Heaven and earth met and overlapped as perfectly as possible. Man's sin broke the world and made it no longer an accurate shadow of heaven. We think that what we can see and touch is what's real. God says otherwise. The things that are able to be seen and touched are temporary and will fade with time. The unseen things are immovable and last forever. The heavenly things, the spiritual things, these are what are real. One day, heaven and earth will be completely reunited. The process is happening right now.

Don't modify the law

We know there must have been revelations that God no longer wishes us to have. Moses's father-in-law, Jethro, was a priest of Midian (Exodus 2:16). And Melchizedek was also a priest of the Most High. How could these men be considered righteous priests without knowing how to make offerings to God appropriately? God must have given them instructions, but God has made it clear through Moses what our current set of instructions is (Deuteronomy 4:2, 12:32).

We do still have the instructions given to the Levites. This is for a purpose. The temple and sacrifices are shadows so we may come to know the true spiritual reality of how to serve God and one another.

Group Discussion Exercise: The Stoning Story

ARTHUR WENT TO THE CITY SQUARE and reported that he had a charge to make. The local judge said he would make a record of it in case any other witnesses came forward.

Four weeks after the incident, Arthur got a call from the judge telling him that two new witnesses had come forward about the same incident and that he needed to come to the square for questioning as soon as possible if he would like to testify. Upon arrival, Arthur and the two others were each directed into three separate rooms. The city official asked Arthur, "You understand that your landlord Mr. Newcomb may be condemned to death by the judge. You agreed four weeks ago that if he is found guilty of a capital offense, you are willing to initiate the execution. If not, you will not be allowed to testify against him. And if we discover that you are lying to us about his guilt, you will receive the penalty he would have received. Is that clear?"

"Yes, I know," said Arthur.

"Okay," said the official, "we have two other people who have come forward about the same incident. Mr. Newcomb is in the next room with several judges. You will be questioned."

In the next room, there were about eighty members of the public who had come to hear the matter. After Arthur very carefully recounted the details for everyone to hear, leaving out anything he was not deathly confident of, the official asked him some questions about the woman he saw his landlord with. They asked if Arthur could identify her from some photos. He showed Arthur photos of twenty different women and asked if he could identify her. Arthur was not certain enough to identify her, only Mr. Newcomb and that the woman was not Mrs. Newcomb. The official asked Arthur if he knew of how the woman might have traveled to the house that evening. Arthur told him about the pink car he remembered. It had been facing away from the house as if it had been backed into the driveway.

After the questioning was over, the official brought in Mrs. Newcomb and the other man who Arthur discovered was Mr. Newcomb's son Finney. Arthur knew they had just received the same reminders that he had been given before entering. As they were being questioned, they shared a different set of details. Arthur learned that Mrs. Newcomb and Finney both knew who the woman was; it was Finney wife, Mr. Newcomb's daughter-in-law. Mrs. Newcomb knew this relationship had been going on for some time, and she had installed cameras in the house that Mr. Newcomb was unaware of. These had alerted them to what was happening that evening, and when they arrived, they witnessed what happened. They confirmed along with Arthur that Finney's wife had a pink car that she had backed in that night during the thunderstorm. All three had witnessed their actions in the bedroom. They were questioned in detail, and their separate testimonies agreed to the judge's satisfaction when they were questioned about surrounding details.

When they were asked why there was a delay in coming forward to testify, they said they were leaving for a long trip the next day which could not be postponed. They came forward immediately upon returning.

After all the questioning was completed, the judges conferred with themselves. The case was highly unusual, and the fact that Finney, Mr. Newcomb's son, was bringing a charge added a complication. The judges talked about the law that gives the death penalty for a child who strikes either of his parents. Finney stoning his father to death, while one judge argued was justified, would also require that he be put to death afterward as another judge argued. They were not exactly sure how to proceed since there was only one qualified witness against both Mr. Newcomb and his daughter-in-law. That was Mrs. Newcomb, Finney's mother.

Their decision was to appeal to a Christian judge for a ruling. He reasoned that while Finney was an eligible witness against his wife, his testimony against his father was not allowed since he was not willing to initiate the execution against his father since that would mean his own death also due to Exodus 21:15. So his testimony against his father was not allowed to stand, only his testimony against his wife, and that God would judge Finney for failing to bear witness against his father. Arthur's testimony did not seek to condemn Finney's wife since he was not confident enough to identify her. So the priest ruled that there were two eligible witnesses against Mr. Newcomb (Arthur and Mrs. Newcomb), and two eligible witnesses against Finney's wife (Finney and Mrs. Newcomb).

The priest gave his decision for this and led Mr. Newcomb and Finney's wife outside to a pit encircled with stones. As they were being led outside, someone who had been present at the trial raised a commotion and disrupted the public. The officials, judges, Arthur, Mr. and Mrs. Newcomb, Finney, and his wife were all jostled about, and a crowd gathered into the pit to block the stoning. The people were so convinced that this was wrong, they started shouting at the judge that the city would take responsibility for whatever had happened so that the judgment could not be carried out on Mr. Newcomb and his daughter-in-law.

Scripture Index

161